Volume XXX: NUMBER ONE
2005

Contents

Modern Psychoanalysis

The editors invite submissions of articles to MODERN PSYCHOANALYSIS. Manuscripts should be typed, double-spaced, on one side of 8½ × 11 inch white paper, or on a 3½ inch disk. The first page should start halfway down from the top. Submissions should be in triplicate with a SASE. Footnotes and bibliographies must conform to the style of this journal. The editors should be informed, with the submission, if the article has appeared or has been submitted elsewhere.

MODERN PSYCHOANALYSIS, the journal of the Center for Modern Psychoanalytic Studies, 16 West 10th Street, New York, NY 10011, is published semiannually. Individual subscriptions are on a yearly basis: $53.00 per year. Institutions: $60.00. Write for foreign rates.

ISBN 0-9764359-5-0   YBK Publishers, Inc., 425 Broome St., New York, NY 10013

MODERN PSYCHOANALYSIS is abstracted and indexed in *Psychoanalytic Abstracts* (Pa. A).

It is with great sadness that we announce the passing of
Phyllis W. Meadow, founding editor
of *Modern Psychoanalysis*, January 19, 2005.

The Death of an Entrepreneur:
A Systematic Analysis
of a Manic Defense[*]

ROBIN POLLACK-GOMOLIN

A 48-year-old man with bipolar disorder was referred for psychoanalysis. Over the course of his treatment, I repeatedly observed that he terminated his associations using different forms of interruption. In the third year of treatment when this dynamic became the central feature of the transference, I began a systematic investigation of this phenomena. My analysis of these modes of interruption indicated that they represented undifferentiated psychic experiences of the patient. They informed me of his urgent need for tension reduction and the risks affect formation posed to his psychic cohesion. The renunciation of secondary processes also symbolized his wish to maintain a symbiotic union with the transference object. The results of my analysis yielded numerous dynamic insights that were essential to understanding this patient's functioning and use of the analytic transference. This knowledge had important clinical implications. It guided my interventions in a manner that moved the treatment beyond a therapeutic impasse and helped the patient and me grow into the many meanings his words were trying to create.

Mr. A was referred to me seven years ago. His psychiatric history includes the diagnosis of a major mental illness and several hospitalizations for psychotic episodes. Married with two children, Mr. A's

*The International Psychoanalytic Association awarded a version of this paper its 2004 Exceptional Contribution to Psychoanalytic Research Award.

upper-class suburban lifestyle had been maintained by his mother who supplemented his wife's income and financed his numerous business ventures, all of which had failed. Upon his mother's death, several months prior to our first meeting, Mr. A's father refused to continue supporting him, insisting that he find employment. Mr. A was clearly unable to handle this imperative. It remains my impression that this unexpected loss of his mother, coupled with his father's demand, reactivated manic symptoms that had until this point been stabilized through medication.

At our first session, Mr. A handed me a computer spreadsheet that annotated his history of relationships. It cross-referenced names to five headings: abuse, neglect, abandonment, betrayal, and loss. He spoke vociferously about having been "victimized" by family, friends, and business associates. It seemed that any individual he had ever known had "orchestrated fraud" or "perpetrated injustice" upon him.

Psychotic and delusional ideation characterized the first three years of Mr. A's sessions. He clung desperately to fantasies of entrepreneurship and a self-image that defined him as a brilliant thinker. He spent his analytic hours describing to me the facets of his genius and various strategies for disseminating his knowledge. He refused to work in what he called the "white-bread world" and spent whatever money he came by creating websites and toll-free numbers—structures that could actualize the many fantasies he spoke of during our sessions. Inevitably, the plans and ideas he had conceived (and, in fact, Mr. A referred to his ideas as his babies) always failed.

During these early years, Mr. A was at his "psychic best" and most integrated when he engaged in a projective dialogue that discharged his intense wrath towards those individuals he believed were sabotaging his brilliance. He expected his wife, children, and members of his extended family to remain loyal to his cherished goal of entrepreneurship and perceived any expectation of him that challenged this fantasy as betrayal. The perception of betrayal intensified his hatred, which had many affective castings: disdain, righteous indignation, disgust, and wanton rage. In the moments when Mr. A accessed some insight into the global nature of his failings, he would be overcome by tremendous depression and talk about suicide. When he spoke about the failure of his entrepreneurship, his feelings of loss were profound. He reminded me of Willy Loman in *Death of a Salesman*. I would receive frantic calls from him, telling me that he was in his car and thinking about driving off a bridge.

Throughout the first years of his treatment, Mr. A frequently stated that he felt empty and I came to learn that his various entrepreneurial identities were attempts to restructure an internal space he often described as a "cavernous vacuum." His communications presented an ongoing dilemma with regard to gender, role, and sexual identity. His mother, having worked, assumed what he believed were masculine obligations. He described his father as a nasty, passive underachiever. To work at a real job represented a wish to be like his mother and become feminized. Entrepreneurship represented an unconscious identification with his father and a striving towards masculine potential. Mr. A was always stuck between these two images, perpetually confused about which to protect and which to abandon.

In terms of his sexual functioning, the mere notion of physical intimacy had frightened Mr. A for many years. His wife, like his late mother, is a large-framed woman. At some point he began to imagine that having sex with her would be like having sex with his mother. Being touched by her would either kill him or contage her with his madness. Sometimes he experienced the desire to kiss or embrace men. However the idea of homosexual sex also disgusted and frightened him. He couldn't penetrate or be penetrated.

In the third year of Mr. A's treatment, whole associations to the past began to replace the manic ideation that had been dominating his dialogue with me. As the presence of these associations increased so did his need to avoid secondary levels of awareness regarding their content. Rather than exploring his words, he would reject them by fleeing back into delusion, fits of projection, or psychotic tirades about world events. Often he would terminate an association by chastising me for failing to "promote" his "entrepreneurial brilliance" and demand that I either explain his associations, tell him what to talk about, or talk about myself. At other times, a variety of physical and somatic activities successfully interrupted these new communications that were becoming very reality based.

Mr. A's avoidance of secondary meaning became the central feature of the transference, and the treatment reached a therapeutic impasse during its third year. Intrigued by what seemed to be my patient's unconscious need to destroy higher levels of awareness, I began to examine the intrapsychic function of this unconscious dynamic. Ramzy (1963) states that in order to make good observations the psychoanalytic researcher must arrive at an exact description of the phenomenon observed and make a complete recording of all the circumstances which may have a connection to them (p. 62). Spotnitz (1969) writes that to be of maximum value to narcissistic patients psychoanalytic investigations have to be conducted empirically (p. 11).

In keeping with these thoughts, I identified the following ways in which my patient interrupted his associations during the analytic hour:

Attack on the association: The patient offers an association and then negates or denies its value, meaning, or relevance to the treatment.

Interrogatory of the analyst: The patient chastises the analyst for failing to cure him, demands that she explain the meaning of an association, talk about herself, or tell him what to talk about.

Fixed delusion: The patient's association is interrupted by a repetitive delusion about a region with two business markets worth billions of dollars. He owns one market and is trying to acquire the second so he can represent both. Upon acquisition of the second market his plan is to merge them into one region.

Projective interruption: The patient engages in an intensely hateful dialogue that demeans and degrades members of his family and other individuals.

Psychotic monologue: The patient's association is interrupted by a highly pressured, fragmented monologue, the duration of which ranges from three to eight minutes. It is unintelligible except for the last fragment, which appears as a recovery link that returns the patient to a more stable mode of associating. An example of the recovery link is, "I better be able to make money in this market or be ready to sell macaroni in Tahiti."

Somatic action: This somatic interruption includes yawning, falling asleep during session, complaints of cramps, body aches, or headaches, or any somatic activity that terminates the patient's associations.

Physical action: The physical interruption includes any motor activity that disrupts an association and enacts thought rather than utilizing language (hand gesturing, singing, rising off the couch, pointing to the analyst).

By studying the style and content of the actual interruptions, the narrative content of my patient's discourse, prior to and following them, as well as my clinical understanding of the data in the context of each session and the entire analysis of this patient, I analyzed the intrapsychic function of these interruptions.

Clinical Discussion

The analysis of the data indicated that each interruption had both an intrapsychic and drive-related function. The *attacks on the association* were organized and coherent. This mode of interruption destroyed the in-the-moment meaning of Mr. A's words and isolated the affects that were contained within them. While the tension from an ego-dystonic experience was obviated, cognitive understanding and the potential for extended awareness (i.e., insight) were sacrificed as a result of this intrapsychic rebalancing.

The *fixed delusions*, like the *attacks on the association*, were for the most part structured units of dialogue. They were, however, issued in a fragmented and more pressured style. Over the course of the analysis Mr. A's reliance upon a manic defense has been lessened. In the first year of his analysis, his discourse was completely dominated by manic delusions. In the second and third years, while still very present within his discourse, the manic need for the delusional material was reduced. This evolution in style seems to be a natural byproduct of following the contact function.

Most of Mr. A's awareness of affects is managed by his body, the pre-ego. It responds to the discharge of tension associated with affect formation through continuous minisomatic and physical acts. At the symbolic level, this was one of Mr. A's business markets (soma). He "owns" and "represents" it. The second market was his cognitive ego (psyche), the benefactor of his associations. This region was barely formed and lacked structure. As Mr. A often told me, "The second market is not mine. I am still trying to acquire it. I don't own it yet." As a result of the lowering of his manic defense, its products (associations) were able to "slip" through the stimulus barrier that separated his two markets, the psyche-soma. Historically this border of perception had been insulated by an active manic defense.

When Mr. A negated the content of his associations, he was pleading with me to give meaning to these products, these escaping pieces of his internal life. In those moments the patient was struggling with the unconscious arousals his associations promoted. My refusal to signify his words and validate his internal life products further compounded his feelings of disassociation. At the level of drive energy, he was struggling with the psychic tension that these associations stimulated as they attempted to cross corporal sensing and make their way into fuller levels of awareness.

If we view Mr. A's associations as sources of great psychic tension, symptoms of fuller consciousness, the psychic value of the delusion is better appreciated. It was a compensatory reference that lay between coherency and fragmentation, a communication that maintained a connection between the psyche and the soma—it bound the tension between these two markets. One was fighting for awareness while the other was fighting to keep awareness preconscious, confined to the primitive senses of the body private. The delusion was a psychic truce, drawn between primary and secondary levels of processing.

The *interrogatory of the analyst* was the first interruption that moved from representational disclosure to an enactive mode of remembering (Loewald, 1976). These interruptions were transference demands. They were not questions that reflected Mr. A's interest in me. In their mildest form they represented a "rapprochement contact" with the object. Mr. A turned back to the analyst for assistance. In their most extreme expression the patient was attempting to bring his aggression into the transference relationship, to humiliate and control the transference object (analyst) who frustrated his demands. The interrogatory was an enactment of a relationship between a powerful object and passive subject in which the latter's extreme dependence and aggression were manifested simultaneously.

The *projective interruption* was also enactive. During the course of his treatment, Mr. A has demonstrated a heavy reliance upon projective discourse. As forms of disclosure these interruptions introduced the patient's failed identity, immature ego, lack of impulse control, sexual naiveté and inadequacy, homosexual longings, powerlessness, and "phantastic" expectations of the object. They relieved him of awareness that would otherwise have overwhelmed his frail ego and promoted the denial of his dependent status.[1]

It was not the narrative content of the projection or its evacuative utility as a defense, however, which initiated its significance within this patient's discourse. It was the impact of the *projective interruption* as a powerful mechanism, a unit of organized destructive affect which signified its "felt" value. What was revealed in this type of interruption was a level of wanton, cannibalistic rage towards the object who was perceived as denying the patient access to unlimited gratification.[2] In many of these interruptions the patient gestured a strangulation, pounding, or beating of this withholding object. At the deepest level of his dynamic unconscious, these associations were instinctual rather than object-laden. They represented a disruption of his complete access to the pleasure principle and to tension-free living.

At the intrapsychic level the object is an unmentalized image of the patient, a cast of his weakest links.[3] Though in the moments of the pro-

[1]As Klein (1935) stated, "That which is first of all denied is psychic reality. The ego may then go on to deny a great deal of external reality" (p. 161).

[2]Fonagy (1991) best describes what this analyst observed: "Absence of concern for the object which may manifest as remarkable cruelty . . . [i]t contains no compelling theory of pain in the object's mind" (p. 63).

[3]This latter observation is in accordance with Kernberg (1991) who states that some patients have "a wish to maintain the relationship with the hated object in an enactment of an object relationship between a sadistic agent and a paralyzed victim" (p. 218).

jection the patient achieved a dominant position in relation to the object, his gross dependency needs still required that he remain affixed to it. Ultimately this unconscious need adjusted the content of the projection, restoring his massive relationship to the object.[4] Hence, the intense demand of his evacuative need. In both the *interrogatory of the analyst* and the *projective interruption* it was observed that there was an increased effort on the part of the ego to reduce the increasing destructivity of the drive and protect the object.

The *psychotic monologues* were actual breaks with reality. During them the patient and I were no longer connected. He retreated fully into the privacy of a psychic split. These interruptions followed associations that revealed that deep within his psyche the patient was confronting his most existential conflicts. The tension of budding awareness regarding psychic differentiation and separateness from the object was overwhelming.

At the manifest level of the discourse, representation of the patient's primary conflict (differentiation from the object equals psychic death) was achieved. However, it vanished through the contemporaneous interruption of *the psychotic monologue*. The patient's mind *never* survived awareness of any association that symbolically communicated separation from the original object. Fonagy (1991) notes that "the absence of a theory of mind must constantly threaten the complete mental separation of self and object" (p. 641). This patient (whose associations suggested that he operated from within the absence of a theory of the mind) responded to the threat of "mental separation" catabolically with a complete breakdown of mental structure.

The interruptions through *physical action* were a nonrepresentational form of disclosure. They were coherent communications that enacted rather than expressed Mr. A's transference wishes. He enacted because he was unable to tolerate the conscious experience of the affects that promoted these gestures: the intense frustration, longing to be cared for, and wish to kill. They remained confined to the realm of primary process. His ego was spared secondary awareness of displeasure. Though Mr. A remained disassociated from the unconscious affects that promoted his actions, they were brought into the session as very live awarenesses.

Unlike other interruptions that alienated the patient's discourse, the physical shifts were additions to his narrative. The patient sang a song that captured his struggle with feeling separate from the analyst. He

---

[4]This scenario was repeatedly observed, suggesting that the *projective interruption* was an enactment of a primary object relationship (as described in Kernberg, 1991).

pointed while ordering me to write down his need for a cheerleader. He gestured his need for praise. He rose off the couch in total defiance when I refused to validate his identity. In these moments Mr. A was in control and asserting himself within his discourse; however he remained unaware of the reproductive aspect of his behavior (Loewald, 1976).

Mr. A's discourse is dominated by somatic processes or, as I have called them, *somatic interruptions*. Massive headaches, light sensitivity, frantic facial tics, backaches, fatigue, yawning, and elevated blood pressure and cholesterol levels constantly beset him. In the earliest years of his treatment, body enactments were also a primary mode of affect expression. He consistently reported that his head felt heavy and that he experienced "massive headaches." "My head feels like it is filled with mud. I have to flog my way through it. I feel pressure when I try to think, like painful electrical charges. It makes me so tired."

If primary process thinking is conceptualized as a contact that represents the undifferentiated mentalization of the pleasure principle (that requires neither organization nor structure), then the cognitive arousal of secondary process thinking can be viewed as the source of Mr. A's cerebral pressure. What he was actively feeling was the psychic tension that accompanied the delay of gratification as undifferentiated affects were being organized in an attempt to reach fuller consciousness. The pain in his head could be understood as ego pangs, the response of a weak structure that was trying to accommodate the growth of awareness.

When Mr. A's psyche was disintegrating or he was being flooded with unconscious negative affect, sleep and its beckoning embrace, yawning, provided the immediate relief that his stressed perceptual system required. Spotnitz (1969) states that "sleep is satisfying, and not only because it is an objectless state: it also anesthetizes hunger pains and dissipates the craving for the object. In short, sleep obliterates tension" (p. 29). The *somatic interruptions* redistributed drive energy from the perceptual lobe of the ego to the soma, relieving it of the task of secondary representation. This displacement resulted in a reduction of pressure upon the patient's ego.

In my opinion, the primitive modes of contact (seven forms of interruptions) that defined Mr. A's clinical discourse suggested that executive functioning was controlled by the body ego. Nuclei of affect, derived from instinctual energy, attempted to escape its management and enter pathways of higher consciousness. These pathways offered them the potential for new expression, their libidinal binding and formation. However, this cleft of consciousness, the stimulus barrier, the divide between somatic and perceptual awareness, is a cleavage within the drive states where instinctual energy is not fused. The data suggested that this patient's ego did not have enough structure to tolerate this dangerous psychic crossing.

The psychoanalytic view, as posited by Freud (1920) in "Beyond the Pleasure Principle," maintained that the first task of the organism is to assess and react to the internal state of excitation buildup and keep stimulation levels to a minimum. Schneirla (1939) identified the precursors of affects in simple forms of life and noted that approaches toward the source of stimulation occur to effectively weak stimulus, whereas withdrawals occur to effectively intense stimulation (p. 502). He further observed that the internal physiological adjustments that accompanied the approach behaviors were typically the sort essential to building the necessary tissues of anabolic processes (i.e., protein synthesis, absorption). The adjustments of the withdrawal responses were catabolic processes, energy mobilizing, and tissue destructive. Hofer (1990) states that these physiological adjustments may be seen as contributing to the states from which affects emerge.

Thus the first enactment of the psyche is a physiological one, an adjustment of drive energy through both constructive and destructive somatic processes. It is plausible that in the case of this patient there was a predisposition to excessive quantities of internal stimulation or that a hypersensitivity to normal levels of excitation existed and was met through withdrawal and an "energy mobilizing" form of regulation. This would imply its immediate discharge from the psychic apparatus.

When the psychic experience of rising tension through a delay of discharge is obviated, the potential for fusion of drive energy is lost. If the organized states from which affects emerge are embedded within a catabolic prototype or if tension levels are excessive, the fate of the tension that accompanies affect formation would be discharged and higher mental processes would be jeopardized.

Bion (1962) emphasized that the dominance of the reality principle is "synchronous with the development of the ability to think and to bridge the gulf of frustration between the moment when a want is felt and the moment when action appropriate to satisfying the want culminates in its satisfaction" (p. 306). He described this as essential to the mind's ability to function within the reality principle. My patient's interruptions of his dialogue were vicissitudes of this primary psychic dilemma.

As seen from the clinical data, when Mr. A approached higher levels of awareness, he responded with a pattern of primitive defenses as manifested through the seven modes of interruption. Within these moments of unconscious choice, he was, as Bion (1962) suggested, trying to bridge the gulf of frustration (the danger of psychic crossing, the cleavage of drive states). His symbolic communications were evocative descriptions of this specific peril and the fate of his psyche: nonexistence. Secondary levels of cognition require a delay in the discharge of instinctual energy. Bion's directive obligates the mind to exist within a state of accumulating tension and survive its nonrelease. Mentalization and the representation of affect is a product of this critical experience, one that in my opinion is well conceived of as the *primal scene of the psyche*. The data suggested that for this patient the act of physiological and psychical differentiation was unconsciously perceived as a dire threat to his existence.

This dynamic step, as described by many writers (Bion, 1956, 1962; Fonagy, 1991; Gaddini, 1982; Green, 1998; Loewald, 1978; Tahka, 1987; Robbins, 1983), facilitates the proliferation of mental structures, the cell division of the mind. Successful completion yields a maturing mental apparatus, one that is increasingly able to contain and manage drive energy through internal processes and libidinal patterns of fusion, the essential prerequisites of higher consciousness. The clinical data strongly suggested that in the case of this patient, this essential intrapsychic achievement was severely compromised.

In the object field of his mind, the patient = the patient + me. The patient – me = 0. (I have purposely symbolized this pre-object interaction). Freud (1925) wrote that "thinking possesses the capacity to bring before the mind once more something that has once been perceived, by reproducing it as a presentation without the external object having still to be there" (p. 237). Symbiotic mental structures (such as this patient's) lack the capacity to bring forth advanced levels of cognition through the development of an observing ego. There is simply not enough structure to allow the subject to venture outside of himself and become the object (receiver) of his own experience. In the data it was seen that with regard to the content of his associations, the patient was unable to contemplate their secondary levels of meaning. He simply could not venture beyond the primary processing of them.

As Freud (1926) indicated, to have and hold a full thought implies that within the field of the mind, the object, or at least the corporal sensation of its presence, is no longer essential to the cohesion of the ego. The field of the mind has matured and divided. The ego and object are no longer one. The proliferation of mental structures has enabled the mind to survive the separation and reproduce the object from a distance. Freud brings to our attention the critical significance of this achievement. The data indicated that in the case of this patient such a separation represented an *untenable* position. Within the transference relationship I was "refound" as a vital piece of his internal mental structure (the benefactor of his mental cohesion). *If he moved me out of his object field, he would be left with the remains of a mind, the 0.* 0 is equivalent to what developmental theorists refer to as the disruption of symbiotic unity (Mahler, 1967).

Within the data, the death of mental structure was repeatedly symbolized as was the patient's existential need to cast me as the "object of his instinct," an organic source who maintained him (Laplanche & Pontalis, 1974, p. 23). His primal need to have me in this way was a consistent feature within the transference. He longed for me to "mentor" and "strategize" him. His words represented a fantasy about the power of my organic material, the host structure he fantasizes himself as part of one global entity. More than anything, my patient needed me to agree with his thoughts, to hate whom he hated, to respond to him on his terms of satisfaction. *This confirmed his existence and was tantamount to knowing he was alive.*

When I urged him to explore his analytic material and didn't analyze him on demand, I left the object field of his mind.[5] He did not have enough mental structure to survive the separation and reproduce me from a distance for solace. Imagine the resounding echo of my departure within his cavernous vacuum. Patient – analyst = 0 = psychosis. On numerous occasions the patient has told me that without sessions he was sure he would become acutely psychotic and require hospitalization. His primitive senses were so attuned to this potential that he frequently told me he could "smell psychosis."

On the other hand, when I offered myself to him he rebuked me. He regularly expressed the longing to have me in his life in a personal rather than professional way and enacted this wish in a variety of ways: extra analytic contact by phone, requests for back-to-back sessions or extra sessions, and paying me at will so "money is not between us." However, when I explored his fantasy of having me, he was unable to conceive of our union.

An archaic drama produced by primitive mental structures seemed to suggest that if he reproduced me as an object in external reality, the consequence would be dangerous to us, a danger so dire that his mind was willing to sacrifice itself in order to negate the affect which might

[5]Spotnitz (1969) states that during the undifferentiated phase of psychic development the only object that is protected is the object in the infant's mind but that at this phase of development the infant is incapable of distinguishing between psychic and material reality. "Moreover what is conceptualized as protection of the object may well be protection of the self, for these representations overlap" (p. 28).

have given rise to such action through thought. It should not be forgotten that this unconscious dilemma was fueled by excessive drive energy that defied fusion. Hence his fantasy around affect formation was highly overdetermined.

Analysis of the clinical data and the transference relationship strongly suggested this patient was unable to tolerate the thought of any object wanting him. *Given that this would have implied their differentiation from each other and negated his unconscious fantasy of their merged existence, this was not surprising.* Herein we see the tenacious hold of his pathology and why the demand for the object's rejection remained so primary to his mental cohesion. When a primitive need for psychic union becomes the basic composite of desire, attempts at satisfaction must be frustrated in order to preserve the object field of the mind.

A Metapsychological Discussion of the Clinical Data

Mr. A is a man who appears to be living an object-involved existence. He has a wife and two children. He celebrates birthdays and holidays. Year after year he makes New Year's resolutions. He takes his sons to soccer games and looks after an ailing father. Sometimes he can work successfully, though never happily, as his dreams of entrepreneurship remain unfulfilled. He attends to his analytic commitment, filling each session with a variety of primitive psychic contacts.

He speaks of longings for an object and a very deep wish to make contact with it. Yet for Mr. A, life remains a continuum of castrated desire. It is about primordial bodily angst and its continuous intersection with a sense of total psychological powerlessness. In session with him, it is impossible to know if and how these two sensations presuppose each other or whether they can even be differentiated (a manifestation of his central conflict). He described this dysphoric awareness as "a feeling inside of me that I am always stuck in. It is quicksand that I can never get out of." In this section several theoretical conceptualizations will be introduced that deepened my understanding of my patient's intrapsychic development and the processes behind this terminal struggle.

Loewald (1980) contends that in the most archaic layers of the mind there is no separation experience leading to differentiation and separateness, only the danger of annihilation when there is disruption of the symbiotic unity (p. 215). Tahka (1987) comments that this undifferentiated mode of psychic experience is premised upon the existential necessity of tension reduction. Displeasure in response to physiological experience of rising tension states does not give rise to psychic representations. Rather, it is dealt with by physiological processes and psychologically empty conditioned reflexes (p. 236). Modern analysis refers to this process as "discharge."

When representations of object and self are derived from a prototype of physiologic relief (undifferentiated, fragmentary registrations of bodily sensations), control of the instincts as internal experiences differentiated from objects will be rudimentary. Mentation or thought will be defined by repetitive, stimulus-dependent enactments of perceptual-motoric-affective patterns that necessitate discharge (Robbins, 1983). Again, it is essential to keep in mind that this body-dominated pattern of contact includes those states of increased tension during infancy that were not dealt with by real or hallucinated forms of discharge and, as such, failed to achieve psychic representation.

Structures of the mind that are initiated into object life within these confines will inevitably operate under the auspices of a pathological organization involving the ongoing use of primitive defense mechanisms. Its primary aim will be to safeguard the ego. In patients with this developmental constellation, the defense utilizes language and requires an object for completion of the discharge process. *Its expression, however, is a physiological enactment of differentiation gone awry, rather than a psychological one with an object proper.* In the transference with such patients, the analyst becomes an object of "usage" in service of tension reduction (Winnicott, 1969).

These theoretical ideas are brought to life within the clinical data. From the moment this patient's analysis began, I became deeply aware of his primal need to live an isolated existence and that his actions unconsciously pursued this imperative. His entitled, primitive level of demand consistently rendered it impossible for any object to sustain a relationship with him. His siblings and extended family members have asked him to refrain from contacting them.

His wife, whom he perceived as a loathsome, torturing object (as a consequence of her own pathology), was the ideal repository for this patient's discharge needs. She was a source of *constant* displeasure for him. There was never a moment in which he viewed her otherwise, suggesting that *her psychic utility to him may well have been that she functioned as a familiar and primitive representation of drive pressure and represented a tension state in which he was psychically and physiologically vested.*

When Mr. A's longings risked themselves psychologically and ventured beyond his internal confines, frustration was the guarantor of their fate. Every object with whom a connection was sought became an "intruder" or an "encroacher." As I observed him during sessions, I noted that even his fantasies could not be released to an object. Gratification was destined to remain autoerotic as a result of severe psychic, cognitive, and affective inhibitions.

Individuals with primitive mental organizations immediately experience the frustrations associated with the failures of their object involvements as aggression. However, it is only *after* the differentiation of the self from object that aggression is capable of being represented as a mental phenomenon (i.e., rage). Primitive mental organizations will experience aggression as "accumulating drive tension, as an affective state and as a strong impetus to action" (Tahka, 1987, p. 242). The only ever known and safe recourse available to manage this primal feeling is its automatic release, achieved through destructive modes of discharge directed against that which is perceived as causing it or bringing it toward representation.

The analysis of data strongly suggested that my patient's interruptions of his discourse were a result of this psychic necessity. Mr. A's associations were to material that often attempted to represent aggression as well as other affects. Since the structural resources of his ego were inadequate to cope with this effort, Mr. A was obliged to resort to a physiologic level of enactment in order to discharge the accumulating drive tension associated with secondary levels of representation.

Green (1998) writes about the difference between thinking and psychical activity. He states that "psychic events are understood as rooted in the body, thoughts without a thinker" as opposed to thinking, which is "a digestion of the mind" (p. 651). My patient's associations are better understood within Green's understanding. They were thoughts without a thinker, thoughts that the patient's ego was unable to survive (digest) awareness of. When the self is sufficiently differentiated from the object, it is able to represent a more effective and mature way to regulate drive energy. It will, as Tahka (1987) noted, become the "bearer of the subjective experience of being alive" (p. 243) and the subject can then "digest" his thoughts safely.

Lacking the "subjective experience" of psychic differentiation, Mr. A's desire to maintain the object within the field of his mind was consistently expressed within his discourse. When he attacked his associations, he was in effect destroying his attempts at representation. He returned to a safe and familiar level of physiological enactment with the original object. His termination of representation obviated our separateness. In those moments we were as Loewald (1980) stated "one global structure" (p. 215).

The clinical data indicated that Mr. A operated from a psychic position that was insufficiently differentiated from the original object. As a consequence, there was damage to a myriad of psychic processes that are essential to cathecting and internalizing the object and that culminate in the development of more mature defenses. He was completely reliant upon early defenses associated with Klein's paranoid schizoid position.

This is essential to understanding the role any object is destined to play in relation to him. Since his ego processes were dominated by the need to regulate displeasure, he was preoccupied by a compulsive need to recreate the "psychic familiarity" of this dominant affective state within every relationship. This unconscious dynamic promoted Mr. A's "cravings" for and his simulation of extreme tension states as well as his repetitive solicitation of the object's rejection.

In addition, perhaps the risk of differentiation compels this patient's celibacy. Freud (1926) questioned the fate of the instinctual impulse generated in the id and speculated that through repression the expected gratification or discharge was converted into unpleasure or unlust (p. 91). He believed that the ego could exercise this influence over the original impulse because of "its intimate connections with the perceptual system," a relationship which he claimed "provide[s] the basis of its differentiation from the id" (p. 92).

When the ego's perception is dominated by a lack of differentiation, the sexual inclinations it promotes remain influenced by accumulated drive tension—the displeasure and unlust that Freud wrote of. Sex is the re-union of subject with object, an occurrence predisposed by an original separation during infancy when the id and ego became differentiated structures of the mind. The analysis of my data indicated that in the case of this patient, this event was not achieved. At the deepest level of his psychic process, Mr. A has never experienced the full discharge of his instinctual tension concurrent with the emergence of his subjectivity.

On many occasions during his analysis, Mr. A has stated, "Sex is a sinister thing. I could get lost in an orgasm and never return." He expressed his "sense" (rather than understanding) that sex is dangerous but was unable to say more about this. "Sex will make me psychotic." Recently, he asked me if brain chemistry changed during an orgasm. Exploration revealed that while he was sure it did, these changes only occurred during an orgasm with an object. It appeared that at an orgasm achieved through masturbation was safe because it would not disrupt his psychic balance. Sex is separation. Sex is the release of overwhelming tension, in this case tension with lethal potential given its instinctual vicissitudes and undifferentiated quality. It is quite plausible that this unconscious dynamic is the basis of Mr. A's abstinence and fear of sex.

Whether sex and separation will result in the death of the object, annihilation of self, or survival of both is yet to be determined. At this point in his analysis, the fate of self and object as differentiated entities roam Mr. A's symbolic order, entering reality as unconscious enactments that are for the most part physiological and delusional.

Conclusion

> Just because I try in general to keep apart from psychology everything that is not strictly within its scope, even biological thought, I wish at this point expressly to admit that the hypothesis of separate ego-instincts and sexual instincts (that is to say, the libido theory) rests scarcely at all upon a psychological basis, but is essentially supported upon the facts of biology. So I shall also be consistent enough to drop this hypothesis if psycho-analytic work itself is to suggest as more valuable another hypothesis about the instincts. So far this has not happened. It may be that when we penetrate deepest and furthest—sexual energy, the libido, will be found to be only the product of a differentiation in the energy at work generally in the mind. (Freud, 1914)

Psychoanalysis with patients like Mr. A implies working below the level of drive fusion. The function of the transference has only one goal, to enable the patient to complete and survive the enactment of his drive states. Although this is the treatment goal for every patient, for those individuals who present with primitive, tenacious pathology, the challenge to provide a safe, therapeutic regression is a continuous one. This is facilitated by analyzing "the energy at work in the mind" and allowing for its full disclosure. Only then, as Freud states, can it acquire the potential for differentiation.

In the case of this patient, we see that the first two-and-a-half years of the treatment were spent accomplishing this task through the presentation of gross delusional material, massive fits of projection, and flights into psychotic monologues. Mr. A used the transference as a self-preservative medium to safely relive and satisfy autoerotic instincts. We might say that his first transferential experience signifies a return to the pleasure principle. His discourse for the most part has reflected the need to discharge tension and maintain the integrity of the object field of his mind.

I entered his disturbance by induction, bearing witness to his efforts to libidinize drive energy and restructure his intrapsychic space. Baker (1993) states that in very damaged patients the analyst's survival of the counter-transference is crucial because she may be the first individual in the patient's life to do so. "The survival is itself an implicit transference interpretation" (p. 1228). My own dreams have often expressed the beleaguered state of the transference and the emotional upheaval that this patient arouses in me (Gomolin, 2002). It is the constancy of the transference relationship that enables the growth of consciousness in patients like Mr. A.

Somewhere during the third year of treatment, Mr. A's need for continuous drive discharge began to delay itself. Mania was no longer totally in control and running away with his ideation. For the first time in his life, the patient began to hear himself aloud and look for himself within his words. As Green (1998) states, "Thoughts are perceived when speech activates the memory traces of words" (p. 657). Mr. A's discourse is no longer just a repetition of psychical events. An attempt to know his thoughts has begun. The analytic treatment will continue to follow the patient's contact and observe how his drives initiate "new psychical action" (Freud, 1914, p. 77). Contacts during recent sessions, as well as changes in the patient's clinical presentation, suggest that he may be seeking a bit of structure and no longer wants, or needs, to use the session for the sole purpose of tension reduction.

The results of my investigation of this patient yielded numerous dynamic insights that were essential to understanding his functioning and his use of the analytic transference. This knowledge had important clinical implications. It guided my interventions in a manner that moved the treatment beyond a therapeutic impasse and helped both my patient and me grow into the many meanings his words were trying to create.

REFERENCES

Baker, R. (1993), The patient's discovery of the psychoanalyst as a new object. *International Journal of Psychoanalysis,* 74:1223–1233.

Bion, W.R. (1956), Development of schizophrenic thought. *International Journal of Psychoanalysis*, 37:344–346.

—— (1962), The psychoanalytic study of thinking. *International Journal of Psychoanalysis*, 43:306–310.

Fonagy, P. (1991), Thinking about thinking: some clinical and theoretical considerations in the treatment of a borderline patient. *International Journal of Psychoanalysis*, 72:639–656.

Freud, S. (1914), On narcissism: an introduction. *Standard Edition.* London: Hogarth Press, 14:67–102.

———— (1920), Beyond the pleasure principle. *Standard Edition.* London: Hogarth Press, 18:3–64.

———— (1925), Negation. *Standard Edition.* London: Hogarth Press, 19:233–239.

———— (1926), Inhibitions, symptoms and anxiety. *Standard Edition.* London: Hogarth Press, 20:87–172.

Gaddini, E. (1982), Early defensive fantasies and the psychoanalytic process. *International Journal of Psychoanalysis.* 63:379–388.

Gomolin, R. (2002), The countertransference dream. *Modern Psychoanalysis*, 27:51–73.

Green A. (1998), The primordial mind and the work of the negative. *International Journal of Psychoanalysis*, 79:649–665.

Hofer, A. (1990), Early symbiotic processes: hard evidence from a soft place. *Pleasure Beyond the Pleasure Principle.* R. A. Glick & S. Bone, eds. New Haven, CT: Yale University Press.

Kernberg, O. (1991), The psychopathology of hatred. *Journal of the American Psychoanalytic Association*, 39S:209–238.

Klein, M. (1935), A contribution to the psychogenesis of manic depressive states. *International Journal of Psychoanalysis.* 16:145–174.

Laplanche, J. & J. P. Pontalis (1974), *The Language of Psychoanalysis.* Donald Nicholson-Smith, translator. New York: W. W. Norton.

Loewald, H. (1976), Perspectives on memory in psychology versus metapsychology: *Psychoanalytic Essays in Memory of George S. Klein.* M. M. Gill & P. Holzman, eds. New York: International Universities Press.

———— (1980), Instinct theory, object relations, and psychic structure formation. *Papers on Psychoanalysis.* New Haven, CT: Yale University Press.

Mahler, M. (1967), On human symbiosis and vicissitudes of independence. *Journal of the American Psychoanalytic Association*, 15:740–763.

Ramzy, I. (1963), Research aspects of psychoanalysis. *Psychoanalytic Quarterly*, 32:58–76.

Robbins, M. (1983), Toward a new mind model for the primitive personalities. *International Journal of Psychoanalysis.* 64:127–148.

Schnierla, T. C. (1939), Theoretical considerations of the basis for approach-withdrawal adjustments in behavior. *Psychological Bulletin*, 37:501–502.

Spotnitz , H. (1969), *Modern Psychoanalysis of the Schizophrenic Patient: Theory of the Technique.* Grune & Stratton. New York, London.

Tahka, V. (1987), On the early formation of the mind: Differentiation. *International Journal of Psychoanalysis*, 68:229–250.

154 Wallis Road
Chestnut Hill, MA 02467
rgomolin@aol.com

Modern Psychoanalysis
Vol. XXX, No. 1, 2005

Aspects of Disintegration and Integration in Patient Speech*

DAN GILHOOLEY

The author describes his research on fluctuating patterns of language disintegration and integration in the speech of 14 psychoanalytic patients during 50 sessions. A lexical measure of narcissistically disintegrated language is developed and applied to the language of these patients to identify speech samples that are comparatively disintegrated versus those that are integrated. Samples of disintegrated speech were found to be associated with high levels of self-reference, negation, emotion, and reflective thought; an emphasis on immediate experience; the loss of function words that connect nouns; a loss of speech diversity; and an emphasis on equivocal expression where the self is represented as discontinuous. Samples of integrated speech were informationally rich narrative descriptions that were highly diverse, employed contexts of past/present and self/other as a means to unify experience, and represented the patient and others as continuous in time. The author concludes by suggesting that cycles of disintegration/integration occuring in patient speech reflect the mind's self-regulating method of adapting to changing internal and external conditions, proposing that psychopathology be conceived as disruptions in this self-regulatory process and that psychotherapeutic treatment be thought of as re-regulating this naturally occurring process.

I'll begin by providing a theoretical overview of my approach to research of patient speech in psychoanalytic sessions. One psychoanalytic perspective of the therapeutic process proposes that within sessions patients unconsciously go through cycles of disintegration and

*The author wishes to thank Wilma Bucci, Robert Marshall, and Stephen Soldz for their assistance in developing the ideas contained in this paper.

integration in which they repetitively fall apart and reassemble themselves in new ways, and through the use of this recurring process, they change. The psychoanalytic theory that broadly encompasses this therapeutic process is called "regression in the service of the ego" (Kris, 1952; Hartmann, 1958). There are four basic aspects of regression that are important to understand in following my research. First, regression is defined as a state of altered consciousness, selectively and temporarily employed for the purpose of responding to changing internal and external conditions. In other words, regression only affects a small portion of the mind at any moment. Second, regression is an entirely unconscious self-regulatory psychological process. Third, my study assumes that regression is closely associated with language disintegration, so I try to study cycles of regression in psychoanalytic sessions by examining patterns of disintegration and integration present in patient speech. While studying these speech patterns, I assume that language and mind are linked so that disintegrated speech represents a (selectively) disintegrated state of mind. Finally, in my research I begin by looking for the *formal* properties of disintegration and integration and, therefore, I examine *how* people speak, not *what* they talk about. For example, my research doesn't attempt to identify speech associated with infantile experience or immature behavior as "regressed," though in psychoanalysis these would qualify as forms of temporal regression. Instead my research is designed to study the formal attributes of disintegrative and integrative speech, based upon the belief that studying the form or style of speech will more clearly reveal how the human mind works. I anticipate that by studying the form of speech, rather than its content, individual differences among speakers will be eliminated and more universal properties of disintegration and integration common to all people will become apparent.

Now let me briefly describe my data and my research methods. The research I'll be discussing in this paper is based upon a computerized analysis of the language (nearly 175,000 words) spoken by 14 patients during a total of 50 psychoanalytic sessions. The patients, seven female and seven male, represent a broad range of psychopathology, from character disorder accompanied by anxiety and/or depression, to somatic symptomology and schizophrenia. All patients were seen in multiple session/week psychoanalyses, and all were being treated by senior clinicians. Psychoanalytic sessions were tape-recorded and then transcribed. Typewritten transcripts were optically scanned into a computer and then coded for use with two computerized text-analysis software systems.

Linguistic Inquiry and Word Count (LIWC) is psycholinguistic text-analysis software developed by the social psychologist James

Pennebaker (Pennebaker et al., 2001). Using this software, I analyzed patient speech for the presence of 30 psycholinguistic variables such as present and past tense; speech diversity; article and preposition use; negative affects such as anger, anxiety, and depression; positive emotions; various qualities of cognition like sensation, certainty, and reflective thought; language associated with the body and symptoms. An advantage to using LIWC is access to a large number of validated psycholinguistic measures. With it I could analyze various samples of text for the presence of particular qualities of speech I wanted to study. Along with Pennebaker's LIWC, I used another piece of software, Discourse Attribute Analysis Program (DAAP), developed by the psychoanalytic process researcher Wilma Bucci (Maskit et al., 2005). Bucci's DAAP software is a state-of-the-art tool designed to analyze language use during psychoanalytic sessions. The distinguishing feature of the DAAP software is that it provides a running average within a linguistic dimension under study and produces a graphical display of the changing frequency of this form of language in the speech of the patient throughout the session. For example, if I wanted to examine the patient's use of angry language, I could select the dictionary of anger words developed by Pennebaker and employ this dictionary in DAAP, which would show me the fluctuating frequency of anger words present in the patient's speech throughout a session. You'll see an example of the DAAP software at work in the next section of this paper.

In conclusion, let me identify the overall goals that have guided my research:

- Develop a lexical measure of disintegrated speech
- Identify characteristics of integrated and disintegrated speech
- Identify qualitatively different kinds of disintegration and integration
- Study patterns of disintegration and integration in the speech of patients during analytic sessions

The first two of these goals, developing a lexical measure and identifying the characteristics of disintegrated and integrated speech, will be discussed in this paper.

Linguistic Ingredients of Disintegrated and Integrated Speech

The relationship between speech and mental illness has a long association with psychoanalysis. Freud's (1891) first professional publication was *On Aphasia: A Critical Study.* Consider, as well, that in the first case in psychoanalysis (Breuer and Freud, 1895), Josef Breuer's patient, Anna O, was a young woman who lost her ability to speak her native German and then turned several languages (Italian, French, and English) into a nearly incomprehensible "word salad" before becoming mute. Breuer's diagnosis of hysteria (or schizophrenia) may cause us to overlook the fact that for much of her treatment with Breuer, Anna O was aphasic. Because Anna O became the first example of the "talking cure," psychoanalysts have concentrated on the curative aspect of her language use, underestimating the extent to which her changing mental condition could be understood through a careful study of her disintegrative language. My point is simply to emphasize that from the beginning of psychoanalysis speech disorder and mental disorder have been closely linked.

I began my research into language disintegration by examining empirical findings in the study of speech associated with a variety of mental disorders: depression (Lorenz & Cobb, 1954; Raven, 1958; Weintraub 1981), schizophrenia (Faber & Reichstein, 1981; Rieber & Vetter, 1995; Barch & Berenbaum, 1997), autism (Tager-Flusberg, 1999, 2000), aphasia (Goodglass, 1993; Bates et al., 2001), dementia (Gerwith et al., 1984; Hier et al., 1985), and stress and fatigue (Leith & Pronko, 1957; Miyake et al., 1994; Blackwell & Bates, 1995; Bard et al., 1996; Bates et al., 2001). As I reviewed this literature, it was interesting to discover that the language of these various forms of pathology all possessed similar disintegrative features that appeared to follow attributes of the egocentric inner speech described early in the last century by Piaget (1959) and Vygotsky (1934), and the properties of diffusion and indefiniteness, lability and syncreticism found in regressed thought described by Werner (Werner, 1940, 1978; Werner & Kaplan, 1984). The basic characteristics common to speech found in depression, schizophrenia, aphasia, autism, and dementia were:

Narcissism: As speech disintegrates, it becomes increasingly egocentric (self-referential) and focused on immediate experience. Along with an increased interest in the self, there is diminished interest in others. There is unnecessary repetition of words and therefore a reduced diversity in speech as well as an increase in negation (e.g., "no," "not," "never").

Relative mutism: Depression, Broca's aphasia, autism, and schizophrenia are all characterized by laconic speech. These patients simply speak fewer words and use shorter phrases and sentences. There is a restriction in the spontaneity of speech as they move toward silence. Indeed, one neurologist (Heir et al., 1985) investigating speech disintegration identified silence as the last stop in speech disintegration, the point at which language ends.

Omitted words: There is omission of some basic words, like articles ("a," "an," "the") "lost" in Broca's aphasia. In both aphasia and schizophrenia, speech bears marked resemblance to the inner speech described by Piaget (1948), Vygotsky (1934), and Werner and Kaplan (1984), which is both laconic and "telegraphic" (i.e., economically compressed).

Diffuse, indefinite speech: In aphasia there is an apparent loss of the ability to find the right word. As a result aphasic speech becomes vague, indefinite, and inexplicit. Schizophrenic speech is characterized as tangential and unelaborated with shifting frames of reference. The schizophrenic appears unable to appropriately shift attention in response to changing external stimulation, so his speech remains highly egocentric.

Uncertainty: Because of the dramatically increased indefiniteness and loss of stable identity that characterize their form of speech, the language of both aphasics and schizophrenics is filled with uncertainty.

Empty verbosity: Both schizophrenia (disorganized type) and Wernicke's aphasia are characterized by an empty, meaningless verbosity often called "word salad." In the field of linguistics, these patients possess the ironic designation of being both "grammatically fluent" and incomprehensible. They appear to have largely lost the ability to comprehend language, and therefore are commonly thought to have "lost their minds." In general, there is an increasing emptiness in the content of disintegrated speech.

Syncretic speech: Researchers propose that in schizophrenia there is a loss of stable identity because there is an absence of certain logical assumptions or certain forms of abstract thinking. This is the basis for describing this disease as a "formal thought disorder." There is a loosening of associations that would otherwise bind ideas, which can result in the production of bizarre delusions or hallucinations. It is this property of speech that makes it a fertile environment for the condensation and displacement typical of primary process speech. Speech is described as fragmented, concrete, and idiomatic.

Having discovered broad similarities within the language associated with very different forms of mental illness, I looked for a way of understanding this underlying commonality. While schizophrenia, dementia, depression, and aphasia are not the same illness, they share a common symptom: the disintegration of language. At this initial stage of my research, "fever" was a metaphor I found to be useful in explaining this underlying commonality of language disintegration. Many different kinds of illness produce a fever in the body. A fever doesn't indicate the presence of a single disease, but rather the condition of inflammation. I wondered if the deterioration of language associated with different forms of mental illness was a kind of "mental inflammation." Was language disintegration functioning like a fever as a restorative effort in the face of an incapacitating mental condition? Certainly the increased narcissism (self-reference) associated with disintegrated speech reflected a turning away from the world and focusing attention on the self. I believed that this increased egocentrism might be an attempt at self-restoration. What about the loss of function words; the increased repetition, indefiniteness, and uncertainty; and the loss of logical structure associated with disintegrated speech? Perhaps the deterioration of language reflected a purposeful breaking of numerous mental connections, truly a destruction of "certainty," that melted the glue holding together an associated group of ideas within the mind, with the goal of creating new connections between memories, thoughts, and feelings; all of this being undertaken in an effort to resolve currently destabilizing forms of internal or external stimulation. This is how this ubiquitous sort of language disintegration looked from the point of view of adaptive regression.

My review of the theoretical and empirical literature on language disintegration led me to propose that a language of regression would contain two central attributes, increased narcissism and increased disintegration, to accomplish two goals: the *maintenance of self* during a process of *self-revision.* I anticipated that narcissism would be expressed in four ways: an increased use of first person singular pronouns (e.g., "I," "me," "my"), a reduced frequency of new or unique words spoken, an increase in equivocal speech, and an increase in negation (e.g., "no," "not," "never"). Narcissism would function in a *conservative* way to maintain the self in the face of destabilizing conditions. High levels of repetition would maintain the status quo, while equivocation would maintain equilibrium between competing desires, wishes, or beliefs. At first I didn't know how to identify equivocation through word frequencies, but eventually I came to connect it with a balanced use of words that *include* (e.g., "also," "and," "with") and *exclude* (e.g., "but," "except," "however"). Within narcissism's conservative frame, negation would be used to express the desire for "*no change.*"

Disintegration, on the other hand, would be reflected in six different ways: increased mutism, increased uncertainty and vagueness, increased negation, the absence of spatial language, a loss of function words used to connect nouns, and a dissociation of thought and feeling. Because my software was unable to track silence, I employed a linguistic measure affiliated with mutism: words per sentence. I assumed that language disintegration would be associated with a reduction in words spoken per sentence. Uncertainty and vagueness would be conveyed in speech that was increasingly tentative (using words such as "maybe," "perhaps," "guess"). Following the linguist Gattis (2001), who suggests that logical thought and spatial language go hand-in-hand, I anticipated finding a relative absence of spatial language (e.g., "above," "around," "down") in disintegrated speech. The loss of function words typically associated with language disintegration would be reflected in a relative reduction in the use of articles ("a," "an," "the") and prepositions (e.g., "as," "for," "with"). In speech disintegration negation would facilitate disintegration and recategorization of thought through use of expressions such as "*not* this." Finally, following the psychoanalytic process researchers Mergenthaler (1996) and Bucci (Mergenthaler & Bucci, 1999), I anticipated that speech disintegration would coincide with the dissociation of feeling and thought; that is, disintegrated speech would be found to contain lots of emotion but little reflective thought, and vice versa.

Having developed a conceptual model of how disintegration might be functioning in a language of regression, I needed to operationalize "speech disintegration" to be able to study the phenomenon in psychoanalytic sessions. At this point I began to create a lexical (word-based) measure of language disintegration. Relying on my review of the theoretical and empirical literatures, I used an idea of "primary traits" as a method for constructing the most elemental measure possible. I believed that if I could pick the parts of speech that were most fundamentally related to the disintegration/integration process, all other associated linguistic qualities would follow in their wake. Both the theoretical and research literatures describe regression as being both narcissistic and disintegrative; therefore, my dictionary focused on narcissistic and disintegrative language, and, indeed, I called it a narcissistic/disintegrative language (NDL) measure. I figured the primary linguistic feature of narcissism would be first person pronoun use ("I," "me," "my"), while the primary trait of disintegration must be the use of negation ("no," "not," "never"). In addition, nonfluency ("uh," "like," "you know") seemed almost by definition to be associated with speech disintegration. So these three primary traits (self-reference, negation, and nonfluency) became the basis of my NDL dictionary. To construct the dictionary, I simply combined the first person pronoun, negation, nonfluency, and filler dictionaries developed by Pennebaker in LIWC. Listed below are the 42 words and several nonfluent phrases that comprise my dictionary.

NDL Dictionary

Aren't	Myself
Can't	Negate
Cannot	Negation
Didn't	Negative
Doesn't	Neither
Don't	Never
Hadn't	No
Hasn't	Nobody
Haven't	None
I	Nope
I'd	Nor
I'll	Not
I'm	Nothing
Isn't	Nowhere
I've	Shouldn't
knowG (coding for "you know"	Uh
and "I don't know" when used	Um
nonfluently)	Wasn't
MM (coding for nonfluent	Weren't
expressions "like," "well,"	Without
"I mean," "whatever," "and	Won't
so forth")	Wouldn't
Me	Zero
Mine	Zip
My	

Having created the NDL dictionary, I then employed this dictionary in Bucci's DAAP system to examine the shifting frequency with which these dictionary words were present in patient speech over the course of analytic sessions. Based on DAAP's graphical representation of the frequency of language use within the session, I identified periods of "high" and "low" NDL word frequencies. I then went into the text of the session transcripts and extracted these specific segments of speech. Using this procedure, I scored the 50 sessions for the 14 patients in my data set, extracting 118 samples of high NDL, or disintegrated, speech and 82 examples of low NDL, or integrated, speech. I then closely studied these speech samples.

A first step in tracking NDL as a clinical phenomenon was to create a numerical value to indicate the degree to which NDL was increasing or decreasing in patient speech. In other words, I wanted to create an NDL score so that I could use my linguistic measure like a ruler to show that one speech sample was quantitatively more or less disintegrated than another. The NDL score obtained by each speech sample is simply the percent of words within a text sample that are also in the NDL dictionary. (In other words, an NDL score of 3 means that three percent of the speech sample is words from the NDL dictionary.) Here are two samples of patient speech, the first quite integrated and the second very disintegrated, illustrating the kind of speech that the NDL measure captures and its corresponding NDL Score:

> He's very irritable, super sensitive after work. Anything I say to him will set him off. Anyway, he did begin to take a bit more responsibility for paying the rent, and I guess he sort of slacked off again, or something happened, and we went through a whole other thing about this, went through another long protracted battle about him being unwilling to assume that responsibility, feeling that he was being used. (NDL Score: 3)

> Uh, I've, uh, not been, uh, feeling good. And, um, uh, uh, you know, didn't sort of like, anyhow, and, I, um, uh, I don't know, sleepy and, uh, the, um, uh, did, uh, oh, the time thing didn't, uh, bring me like a relief, uh, control of myself, um, um, it doesn't seem to fall into places. Um, uh, it's, uh, sort of strange. And I, uh, I, it's just that I don't understand what's happening to me. (NDL Score: 42)

I think that these two samples demonstrate that the NDL measure captures speech that is highly fractured and distinguishes it from a more integrated kind of speech. To give you an idea of the variation in patient speech in a single session, here is the graphical representation created in DAAP of the presence of NDL in Ms. B's speech in one analytic session. The peaks along the curve represent a high concentration of words from the NDL dictionary, while valleys reflect a correspondingly low presence of NDL speech. The speech occurring at the three highest and two lowest points were selected for analysis and are displayed below.

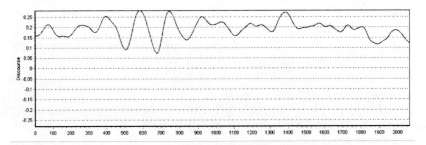

Figure 1. DAAP's analysis of the Frequency of NDL in the Speech of Ms. B in a Session

Session Summary: Ms. B is a married mother of a young daughter. Aggressive and very angry, she feels constrained by both her marriage and her treatment. Based on the six sessions included in my sample, I assessed her as having a borderline personality. The patient had called the analyst on the morning of this session to say that she was sick and that she intended to cancel; the analyst told her to come to the session anyway. She begins the session by telling the analyst that she wasn't really sick but felt that coming to the session would be a waste of time. She says she feels trapped; she wants to be free of the responsibilities of her treatment and her marriage. She says she doesn't want to learn about herself; she wants to make a mockery of the analyst and the analysis; and she wants to sexually tease the analyst and seduce him. When she feels like seducing the analyst, she thinks about quitting treatment. The patient concludes the session by talking about her desire to have an affair to shock her husband, to get more attention from him and the analyst, or to get her husband to end their marriage and free her from the responsibility of making a good marriage and creating a happy family.

Ms. B Disintegrated Speech 1
[about her husband's recent interest in his secretary] . . . upset that, that my husband might be unfaithful to me, or not liking that he was interested in her. I mean, I was concerned about that. I don't know. Maybe, I don't know. I was just thinking about, I don't know. Maybe I'm concerned about having; I don't know. I'm just mixed up now. (NDL score: 33)

Ms. B Integrated Speech 1
You see I was watching this movie yesterday on TV. I was watching this movie about this blonde actress. I don't know why I'm wanting to get the hell out of here. She was in this guy's arms and he was, it was a theatre thing and she was supposed to play seductress and he said, the director that was telling them how to do the scene, he was telling him to whisper in her ear. (NDL score: 6)

Ms. B Disintegrated Speech 2
I don't know. Uh, I don't know. I guess I thought, I don't know. I don't know. I guess I thought that I was wanting to do that with you or, uh, uh, thinking about wanting to turn you on, or, and then I would feel like I would have to leave, quit therapy. You know, I just feel, I guess I just feel like I can't, that it's wrong for me to feel this way. (NDL score: 34)

Ms. B Disintegrated Speech 3

But, I don't know, I just feel like I'm not getting anywhere like this. Like, I told you what happened this morning, my dream, you know, what happened when I tried to remember my dream. I don't know. Maybe I'm just pissed because you're not interested in me. I just feel like, I don't know. I'm feeling stressed out about yesterday because I don't understand what really happened yesterday and what your opinion is. I can't figure it, I can't figure it out. I don't know. (NDL score: 32)

Ms. B Integrated Speech 2

I feel better about him when I'm apart from him. I don't know the reasons for wanting to have an affair. Well, if I had an affair, or if I was unfaithful, does he get mad at me and leave me and take the kids, and then I wouldn't have to be responsible for making this a good marriage and a happy family? But that goes round and round in circles. (NDL score: 15)

In this example of a session with Ms. B, the NDL measure seems to differentiate a disintegrated form of speech from a kind of language that appears to be more integrated. The primary trait method I employed in creating the NDL measure appeared to work. That is, a dictionary based only on "I," negation, and nonfluency did capture language that is also more tentative, more redundant, focused on immediate experience, with significantly fewer function words, and fewer words per sentence. There are two additional qualities present in these samples from Ms. B that are characteristic of the disintegrated and integrated speech I've studied: statements of "self-assessed disintegration" in disintegrative texts and an emphasis on the "other" in integrated speech. You may have noticed in the disintegrated speech samples above that Ms. B says of herself, "I'm just mixed up now," "I can't figure it," and "I just feel that I can't, that it's wrong for me to feel this way." In each instance Ms. B describes her difficulty integrating thoughts and feelings. These sorts of self-assessments are typical of the disintegrative speech identified by the NDL measure, and in my view they offer prima facie evidence that the NDL dictionary does capture speech representing a disintegrated state of mind. A second basic characteristic present in these examples is the association of integrated speech with the "other." In her more integrated language Ms. B is focusing on someone other than herself. That is, Ms. B is talking about "she" or "him." This is fairly characteristic of integrated language, which is often a narrative description about others.

My study of the 118 samples of disintegrated speech and 82 examples of integrated speech from my 14 patients produced the following findings:

- The NDL measure based on negation, nonfluency, and self-reference distinguishes language that is highly fragmented, tentative, and redundant from language that is integrated and diverse. Disintegrated speech is expressed in the present tense and is filled with a combination of high affect and reflective thought.
- Function words (articles and prepositions) that connect nouns and verbs in meaningful ways disappear in disintegrated speech and reappear in integrated speech. Expressed differently, the "connective tissue" or "glue" linking representations of people and things is lost in disintegrated language and reappears in integrated speech.
- Disintegrated speech frequently contains self-reflective statements in which patients comment on their mental state. For example, patients say, "I'm all mixed up," "I can't fit it in," "I'm thinking about something pretty unclearly," or "I feel emotionally distant from myself."
- Disintegrated speech contains large measures of both affect and reflective thought; conversely, in integrated speech words associated with emotion and cognition are comparatively infrequent. In disintegrated speech individuals comment frequently on their thinking, often in negative ways: "I don't know," "I can't remember," "I don't think."
- Disintegrated speech often contains a relatively proportional balance of words that *include* and words that *exclude*, resulting in equivocal or ambivalent speech. Integrated speech, by contrast, invariably contains more words that include. Here are two passages of disintegrated speech representing equivocal speech in which **inclusion** and *exclusion* words are highlighted:

Like, because then, I was thinking, like, why, why did I do *that*, you know, what was I really getting angry about? **And**, like, I don't, I can't believe *that* it was because of coming **here**, **and** stuff that we were discussing. **And** then I realize, like, last night, you know, Bill probably really wanted sex, *although* he wasn't pushing it. *But* he was being awfully friendly.

Should I live **in** the suburbs, *or* where should I live? You live **in** a nice town, *but* a small house . . . **And** then, obviously, it takes a long time to save for a down payment, *but* not *that* long.

These two examples demonstrate how the symmetrically balanced use of inclusion and exclusion words conveys an arrested, immobilized state of mind.

- Transference (both object and narcissistic varieties) is common in disintegrated speech and mostly absent in integrated speech.
- "Control" is a dominant theme in disintegrated speech. Patients seek to control others and events or to control their thoughts and feelings; patients feel controlled by others, events, or their thoughts and feelings; or they simply feel out of control.
- Integrated speech contains a proportional balance between past and present tense verbs. This balanced proportion of tenses is most often expressed by the patient in the use of the perfect verb form to describe *continuous action over time*, as in these examples: "I didn't want to say," "it made me feel," "I haven't heard." Continuity of action in time appears to be a significant component of integrated speech and thought, and this continuity brings a sense of psychological unity to integrated speech.
- Past tense is prominent in integrated speech and conspicuously absent in disintegrated speech. In integrated speech individuals use the past to provide a context through which to understand themselves and others. This process of contextualizing becomes a second unifying aspect of integrated language.

Within these results two fundamental findings are of particular importance. First, the process of disintegration/integration is governed by the shifting flow of two clusters of linguistic attributes that I call "glue" and "solvent." Secondly, psychological qualities of integration and disintegration parallel language disintegration.

Articles, prepositions, and inclusion words form the lexical glue that binds together thoughts and feelings. Prepositions and inclusion words depict how nouns are connected, and for this reason, I've described these function words as the "connective tissue" of language. Pennebaker (2002) calls these words the glue that binds together language and thoughts. What is significant is that this glue "washes out" of language in disintegrative phases and reappears in states of integration. Of course, this makes perfect sense when considering language use from the perspective of the adaptive regression model described in this paper. If the purpose of language is to form a new idea or awareness, then the objects of experience must be combined in new ways. For this new combination to take place, it's necessary to break the existing connections, hence the disappearance of these function words.

Self-reference and negation, combined with high levels of emotion and reflective thought focused in the present tense, become the lexical solvent used to dissolve the glue linking thoughts and feelings. As articles, prepositions, and inclusion words diminish in frequency in disintegrated

speech, there is a corresponding increase in self-reference, affect, negation, and present tense. Returning to the adaptive regression model, it
again makes perfect sense that as the individual becomes increasingly
focused on an immediate personal experience, with heightened emotion
and with the conviction that something is not right or is not known, this
feeling state creates the conditions for a reduction in the linguistic glue
that stabilizes thought. That is, the conditions are now right for a new
thought, a new awareness of feeling, or a new explanation. In these disintegrative phases, the connections between the objects of thought are loos-
ened through the reduction of function words and through the increase in
self-referential negation that repeatedly asserts "what I'm not" as the individual struggles to create new forms of integrated structure.

Finally, it's very important to emphasize that the linguistic properties
of integration and disintegration found within patient speech correspond to the patient's state of psychological integration or psychological disintegration. Within integrated speech the representation of time
plays a central role in psychological integration. Simply put, *in integrated speech, time is the recurring unconscious theme.* In integrated
speech, time serves as a psychologically integrative force in two ways:
through representations of self and other as continuous and through a
process of contextualization in which present experience is interpreted
through the past.

Highly integrated speech emphasizes the continuity of personal
action through time. In this integrated state individuals "*have been* hungry," are "*being* silly," or are "*in* disagreement." In this last example the
patient doesn't say, "We disagreed," to represent a disagreement that
has come and gone. Rather the patient describes himself in the midst of
an *enduring state* of disagreement. Winnicott (1974), in one of his last
papers, "Fear of Breakdown," describes the unconscious fear we all
have of death as an interruption of self in time. Seen from this point of
view, the persistent representation that we find in integrated speech of
a self continuing in time seems to defend against that deeply rooted
unconscious fear we all possess: mortal disintegration. In some forms
of integrated speech, time is central to the creation of psychological
integration in yet another way: through a process of contextualization.
Here present experience is understood in terms of the past, and self is
understood in comparison to others. By using a process of contextualization, patients gain perspective on their unique forms of illness or
observe others' behavior to create a context through which to interpret
their own experience and actions.

The psychological qualities of disintegrated speech involve emphasis
upon immediate experience, self-reference and narcissism, ambiva-

lence, and transference, with each of these qualities contributing to the state of psychological disintegration experienced by the patient. Disintegrated speech always emphasizes immediate personal experience. By focusing on immediate experience, patients stop representing themselves as continuous and keep representations of the self and objects outside the context provided by past and future and, therefore, outside the integration such a context facilitates. One of the most significant qualities of disintegrated speech is the patient's representation of self as discontinuous; I suspect this is the reason why this kind of speech contains a high level of anxious language. Disintegrated speech focuses on the self and on patients' exclusive concern with their personal experience contributes to their state of psychological disintegration. Disintegrated speech is filled with ambivalent conflict expressed through equivocal speech. Ambivalence keeps the patient in a static state and blocks movement toward psychological integration. Transference is a characteristic of disintegrated speech and very rarely occurs during periods of integration. Transference prevents patients from experiencing others and the world as they really are, distorting experience through a process of narcissistic projection. As yet another manifestation of narcissism, transference contributes to psychological disintegration.

Therapeutic Cycle of Disintegration and Integration and Implications for Treatment

Studying cycles of disintegration and integration in patient speech through the lens of adaptive regression has provided me with a new perspective on psychoanalytic process. Recognizing this cycle of disintegration and integration as an aspect of a naturally occuring self-regulatory change process has led me to rethink psychopathology and psychotherapeutic treatment.

If one accepts that the alternating states of disintegration and integration represent a naturally occuring therapeutic cycle, a form of regression in the service of the ego, then this has implications for how we envision psychoanalytic treatment. First of all, if we accept that these alternating forms of disintegration and integration are the mind's natural self-regulating method of responding to a dynamically changing world, then psychopathology can be understood as a breakdown in this self-regulatory system. In other words, the mind's built-in mechanism for adaptive change has failed to meet the challenges imposed upon it.

In these situations failures in the therapeutic cycle are of two basic types: excessive disintegration with too little integration and excessive integration with too little disintegration. Simply put, patients whom we describe as depressed or schizophrenic might be said to suffer from excessive disintegration combined with a relative absence of integration. Patients whom we describe as anxious or obsessive might be said to suffer from excessive integration, combined with an inability to freely disintegrate. The therapeutic process then becomes one of fostering the further development of, or perhaps re-regulating, the patient's natural self-regulating system. Seen from this perspective, certain psychoanalytic conceptions of efficacious treatment appear more compelling than others. For example, interventions that emphasize the capacity to "say everything" and to comfortably *free associate* appear more effective than mutative, insight-oriented interpretations that "make the unconscious conscious." Modern psychoanalytic techniques recommended by Spotnitz (1969) such as joining, mirroring, and reflecting, along with concepts like "saying everything" and "progressive communication," seem well matched to assisting patients to develop a more effective therapeutic cycle. My point is that understanding, no matter how advantageous, has much less therapeutic value than an increasing ability to spontaneously say everything.

My research on disintegrative and integrative processes has led me to emphasize the importance of the cycle of disintegration and integration and to discount the value of individual states of disintegration or integration. To remain in a state of either disintegration or integration for long is dangerously self-destructive. My research suggests that mental health is associated with a supple therapeutic cycle, not with a state of integration. As is well known to any psychoanalytic reader, "disintegration" is as pejorative an expression as "regression," while "integration" is widely viewed to be what we all aspire to. I think this is a mistake. I recommend that when we think about effective treatment, we place value upon the quality, frequency, or depth of the therapeutic cycle rather than either of its end points.

Drive Theory and the Therapeutic Cycle of Disintegration and Integration

If we consider that Freud regards life and death drives as ever present, their interplay shaping every aspect of human existence, then it follows that we should be able to find evidence of such drives in patient speech. Furthermore, we would anticipate disintegrative speech to be associated with a destructive impulse and integrated speech to be linked with constructive forces that promote increased unity. The two speech samples below, spoken by one patient in a psychoanalytic session, show how this therapeutic cycle of disintegration and integration, and the process of regression in the service of the ego, can be understood in terms of drives.

> Sorry I'm late. I had lunch with Joe yesterday and we were discussing a meeting that he had attended during the morning. It was about relating to women and the work place and, you know, women's concerns working in a professional environment. And we started discussing the affirmative action agenda at the college, and I suppose I, well, we were in conflict about it.

> I, I'm not sure what to think about it right now, my thoughts about it. I, I think this gives me a feel—, a reason to feel or believe that I'm being unfairly treated or discriminated against. There is a bit of truth in that, but I don't understand why I feel excited by it. I hadn't really been thinking much about the conversation I had with Joe last night, and I wasn't thinking about it before com—, before just walking in the door and lying down on this couch. I, then it came back to me in a rush, whatever feelings I had. I'm not sure what, I'm not sure what my feelings are all about.

I think that it's fairly obvious that the second passage is more fractured and disintegrated than the first, more filled with self-reference, negation, and uncertainty, and more frequently spoken in the present tense. By contrast, in the first passage the patient is talking about her boyfriend Joe and a disagreement they had had. The subject of this passage is, at least in part, the boyfriend rather than the patient. Furthermore, along with an absence of negation, most of this passage is spoken in the past tense.

Freud (1925), in his paper "Negation," describes "No" as the direct expression of the death instinct:

> The polarity of judgment appears to correspond to the opposition of the two groups of instincts that we have supposed to exist. Affirmation—as a substitute for uniting—belongs to Eros; negation—the successor to expulsion—belongs to the instinct of destruction. The general wish to negate, the negativism that is displayed by some psychotics, is probably regarded as a sign of a defusion of instincts that has taken place through the withdrawal of the libidinal components. (p. 239)

From Freud's point of view, that which unites is the product of Eros, the life force, while negation is the direct expression of Thanatos. When we examine the two samples of patient speech more carefully for evidence of uniting and negating properties we find the following: the more disintegrated passage reveals evidence of *self-reference* and **negation** as highlighted.

> *I, I*'m **not** sure what to think about it right now, *my* thoughts about it. *I, I* think this gives *me* a feel—, a reason to feel or believe that *I*'m being unfairly treated or discriminated against. There is a bit of truth in that, but *I* do**n't** understand why *I* feel excited by it. *I* had**n't** really been thinking much about the conversation *I* had with Joe last night, and *I* was**n't** thinking about it before com—, before just walking in the door and lying down on this couch. *I*, then it came back to *me* in a rush, whatever feelings *I* had. *I*'m **not** sure what, *I*'m **not** sure what *my* feelings are all about.

The strong presence of negation in disintegrated speech is certainly consistent with Freud's perspective on drive derivatives: disintegration and negation appear to go hand in hand. Certainly in my research negation played a prominent part in the corrosive solvent nature of disintegrated speech described above.

From Freud's perspective, the life drive should be about affirming, adding, combining, and unifying. Using the more integrated passage as an example, there are two ways this unifying process occurs in integrated speech. First, there is an increase in the use of articles, prepositions, and inclusion words that link thoughts. These "function words" are the glue that binds ideas together. A second unifying element, appearing in this passage, is the representation of time as "continuous" through the increased use of perfect ("have been") and progressive verb aspects ("was going"). This kind of representation of time "affirms" the individual's continuing existence.

First let's look at this integrated passage with **articles**, *prepositions*, and *inclusion* words highlighted.

> Sorry I'm late. I had lunch *with* Joe yesterday *and* we were discussing **a** meeting that he had attended *during* **the** morning. It was *about* relating *to* women *and* **the** work place *and*, you know, women's concerns working *in* **a** professional environment. *And* we started discussing **the** affirmative action agenda *at* **the** college, *and* I suppose I, well, we were *in* conflict *about* it.

The increased presence of prepositions and inclusion words brings unity to the text.

A second way that this more integrated speech sample gains unity is through the use of past perfect verb aspect (e.g., "have been," "had thought"), and present and past progressive verb aspects (e.g., "am thinking," "was walking"). Unlike "tense," which locates a verb in time in absolute terms (simply as past or present), "aspect" refers to the way the action is represented in time. In general, progressive and perfect aspects characterize events in time in three ways: they are used to represent a past event in terms of the present (e.g., "have been"); they are used to represent actions continuing through time (e.g., "am thinking"); or, in the case of the past perfect aspect, they are used to place past events in sequence (e.g., "had attended"). The large majority of integrated speech samples identified in my research contained numerous examples of these perfect and progressive aspect verb forms. Here is the more integrated speech sample with **perfect** and *progressive* aspect verbs highlighted.

> Sorry I'm late. I had lunch with Joe yesterday and we *were discussing* a meeting that he **had attended** during the morning. It *was* about *relating* to women and the work place and, you know, women's concerns *working* in a professional environment. And we *started discussing* the affirmative action agenda at the college, and I suppose I, well, we were in conflict about it.

As this example makes clear, the purpose of the progressive verb aspect is to describe action as *continuous over time* (e.g., "were discussing"), while the past perfect form ("had attended") is used to indicate an event preceding their conversation. In addition to these verbs the prepositions "in" and "during" also convey a sense of continuous time. The expression "we were *in conflict*" describes a state of *continuing* disagreement, rather than a conflict that has come and gone.

Finally, there is an ironic quality to the application of Freud's drive theory to these two examples of patient speech. Many, if not all, readers will find the disintegrated passage above that is filled with negation—that is, filled with the direct expression of the death instinct—to be more "lively" than the integrated passage. The disintegrated passage exudes the struggle of trying to arrive at some new understanding, while the more integrated passage seems emotionally flat in comparison. Recognizing this irony is central to integrating Freud's drive theory to the later psychoanalytic theory "regression in the service of the ego." Here regression or disintegration is undertaken *in the service of the ego* to create new life, new understanding, new and better adaptation to a changing world. I suggest that in Freud's terminology this sort of disintegrated language contains a *fusion of drives*, where the destructive impulse is employed at the behest of Eros to create new forms of integration.

A Dream

I conclude this paper with a description of a recurring dream of mine that reveals the emotional basis of my research. Throughout my psychoanalysis I've repeatedly had a dream about renovating a very large building that I think of as the perfect art studio. My original training is in the visual arts, and I've been making art all my adult life. Part of being an artist is to be in perpetual pursuit of the perfect studio space in which to create your work, and I've always associated my dream of this big building with my quest for the ideal creative space. The barn-like structures in my dreams are always very large buildings with ceilings 30 feet above the floor that span vast open spaces. The structures are old, a bit dilapidated, and needing repair, but when I come upon them in my dreams they are in the middle of an extensive renovation. Walls have been torn out, steel I-beams are being installed, and portions of the roof and walls are always missing, allowing me to see patches of blue sky laced with dark tree branches. It always feels right to have these large, if unexpected, holes in the building that let the outside in, and I frequently consider how I can retain these openings so that the renovated building will continue to bring nature inside my space. In my dream I walk through these spaces with a feeling of surprise and delight, coming upon newly designed spaces that surprise me with their unexpected potential. I feel like Frank Lloyd Wright climbing through the half-finished construction at Fallingwater. In the early years of my analysis, I found myself climbing through these buildings, inspecting them, but more recently I've become the foreman of an anonymous work crew. The renovations are now too substantial for me to do them alone. Having always associated these dreams with my psychoanalytic efforts to rebuild myself, these dreams invariably fill me with hope and I awaken feeling inspired.

In a recent version of this dream, which I had a few days before presenting my research at a conference, I was in the basement of one of these large structures. We had successfully installed a new foundation underneath an addition that we had quickly, if unexpectedly, attached to one end of the building. Now that the foundation was in place and the addition completed, I set about excavating a remaining mound of earth in the basement. Once I removed this bit of earth, I'd pour a new concrete floor extending the basement under the newly built addition. Looking at this large mound of soil, I realized that it had been sliced perfectly into bricklike chunks, making it very easy to remove. In fact, its removal, to my surprise, was effortless.

I woke up. In a semiconscious state I sat in the dark at the edge of the bed, groping sightlessly for my glasses, realizing that the precisely sliced bricks of earth I'd been excavating in my dream bore a marked resemblance to the 100-word speech segments chopped up by my text-analysis software. I got up, and as I walked through the darkened house moving by familiar feel, I realized that the dilapidated structures I'd been excitedly renovating in my dreams were just like the broken down structures of the disintegrated speech I'd been unearthing in my research. Both were structures in the midst of renovation, replete with partially constructed areas and missing components, filled with surprising additions and new possibilities. Walking through that darkened hallway, I realized that in my research I have been looking for what I'd been dreaming about for the past 25 years: that creative space where art, ideas, and new life find their first breath.

REFERENCES

Barch, D. & H. Berenbaum (1997), Language generation in schizophrenia and mania. *Journal of Psycholinguistic Research,* 26:401–412.

Bard, E. et al. (1996), The DCIEM map and task corpus: spontaneous dialogue under sleep deprivation and drug treatment. *Speech Communication,* 20:71–84.

Bates, E. et al., (2001) Language deficits, localization and grammar: evidence for a distributive model of language breakdown in aphasia patients and neurologically intact individuals. *Psychological Review,* 108:759–788.

Blackwell, A. & E. Bates (1995), Inducing agrammatic profiles in normals: evidence for the selective vulnerability of morphology under cognitive resource limitation. *Journal of Cognitive Neuroscience,* 7:228–257.

Breuer, J. & S. Freud (1895), Studies on hysteria. *Standard Edition.* London: Hogarth Press, 2:1–305.

Bucci, W. (1997), *Psychoanalysis and Cognitive Science: A Multiple Code Theory.* New York: Guilford Press.

Faber, R. & M. Reichstein (1981), Language dysfunction in schizophrenia. *British Journal of Psychiatry,* 139:519–522.

Freud, S. (1891), *On Aphasia: a Critical Study.* E. Stengel, translator. New York: International Universities Press.

———— (1925), Negation. *Standard Edition.* London: Hogarth Press, 19:233–239.

Gattis, M. (2001), Space as a basis for abstract thought. *Spatial Schemas and Abstract Thought.* Cambridge, MA: MIT Press.

Gewirth, L. et al. (1984), Altered patterns of word associations in dementia and aphasia. *Brain and Language,* 21:307–317.

Goodglass, H. (1993), *Understanding Aphasia.* San Diego, CA: Academic Press.

Hartmann, H. (1958), *Ego Psychology and the Problem of Adaptation.* Madison, CT: International Universities Press.

Heir, D., K. Hagenlocker & A. Shindler (1985), Language disintegration in dementia: effects of etiology and severity. *Brain and Language,* 25:117–133.

Kris, E. (1952), *Psychoanalytic Explorations in Art.* Madison, CT: International Universities Press.

Leith, W. & N. Pronko (1957), Speech under stress: a study of its disintegration. *Speech Monographs,* 24:285–291.

Lorenz, M. & S. Cobb (1954), Language patterns in psychotic and psychoneurotic subjects. *American Medical Association Archives of Neurology and Psychiatry,* 72:665–673.

Maskit, B., W. Bucci & A. Roussos (2005), Capturing the flow of verbal interaction: the Discourse Attributes Analysis Program. Paper submitted, *Computational Linguistics.*

Mergenthaler, E. (1996), Emotion-abstraction patterns in verbatim protocols: a new way of describing psychotherapeutic processes. *Journal of Consulting and Clinical Psychology,* 64:1306-1315.

———— & W. Bucci (1999), Linking verbal and nonverbal representations: computer analysis of referential activity. *British Journal of Medical Psychology,* 72:339–354.

Miyake, A. et al. (1994), A capacity approach to syntactic comprehension disorders: making normal adults perform like aphasic patients. *Cognitive Neuropsychology,* 11:671–717.

Pennebaker, J. (2002), What our words say about us: toward a broader language psychology. *Psychological Science Agenda,* 20:8–9.

———— M. Francis & R. Booth (2001), *Linguistic Inquiry and Word Count: A Computerized Text Analysis Program.* Mahwah, NJ: Erlbaum.

Piaget, J. (1959), *Language and Thought of the Child.* London: Routledge and Kegan Paul.

Raven, C. (1958), Verbal dysfunctions in mental illness. *Language and Speech,* 1:218–225.

Rieber, R. & H. Vetter (1995), *The Psychopathology of Language and Cognition.* New York: Plenum Press.

Spotnitz, H. (1969), *Modern Psychoanalysis of the Schizophrenic Patient.* New York: Grune and Stratton.

Tager-Flusberg, H. (1999), A psychological approach to understanding the social and language impairments in autism. *International Review of Psychiatry,* 11:325–334.

——— (2000), Understanding the language and communicative impairments in autism. *International Review of Research in Mental Retardation: Autism.* L. Glidden, ed. San Diego, CA: Academic Press.

Vygotsky, L. (1934), *Thought and Language.* Cambridge, MA: MIT Press.

Werner, H. (1940), *Comparative Psychology of Mental Development.* New York: International Universities Press.

——— (1978), The organismic-developmental framework. *Developmental Processes: Heinz Werner's Selected Writings.* Vol. 1. New York: International Universities Press.

——— & B. Kaplan (1984), Linguistic characterization of objects in external versus internal speech. *Symbol Formation: An Organismic-Developmental Approach to the Psychology of Language.* Hillsdale, NJ: Lawrence Erlbaum.

Weintraub, W. (1981), *Verbal Behavior: Adaptation and Psychopathology.* New York: Springer Publishing Company.

——— & H. Aronson (1967), The application of verbal behavior analysis to the study of psychological defense mechanisms, IV: speech pattern associated with depressive behavior. *Journal of Nervous and Mental Disease,* 144:22–28.

Winnicott, D. W. (1974), Fear of breakdown. *International Review of Psychoanalysis,* 1:103–107.

46 N. Howells Point Road
Bellport, NY 11713
gilhooleyd@aol.com

Toward a Psychobiology of Desire: Drive Theory in the Time of Neuroscience*

MARY SHEPHERD

This paper traces the concept of desire and its meaning in normal discourse through its use in psychoanalysis to some of the findings of affective neuroscience. Recent neuroscientific discoveries about how the brain works are compared with a psychoanalytic view of mental functioning to determine if they are compatible and to understand how they may inform the work of the analyst.

Since the 1980s, when new discoveries in neuroscience began to appear in *Time* magazine and the *New York Times*, I have been fascinated by what seemed to me to be obvious corroboration of fundamental Freudian theory. I became increasingly impressed with the biological grounding of modern psychoanalysis and more and more convinced that psychoanalysis was a natural science in search of empirical verification. In chapter four of *Modern Psychoanalysis of the Schizophrenic Patient*, "A Neurobiogical Approach to Communication" (first formulated in the first edition of this work in l969), Spotnitz (1985) writes: "[T]he curative process entails, in neuroscientific terms, the reversible deactivation of certain neuronal pathways and the activation of new pathways . . . these . . . can be accomplished through either psychological or chemical measures, or through a combination of both" (p. 81).

*This paper is based on a talk presented at the annual Cape Cod Conference of the Boston Graduate School of Psychoanalysis, Wellfleet, MA, *Liberating Desire,* July 31–August 6, 2004.

© 2005 CMPS/*Modern Psychoanalysis*, Vol. 30, No. 1

And, "One unit of communication . . . would be the equivalent . . . of a mouthful of milk" (p. 107). My work with psychotic patients only deepened my conviction that psychoanalysis was grounded in biology. I became more and more convinced. The bizarre behaviors and terrifying quantities of energy in the room left me little doubt that levels of stimulation and states of comfort and discomfort were the most important phenomena I had to work with. How to help transform this bundle of toxic energy into a mind I could understand was a formidable challenge, but the new methods I was learning addressed these problems and left me little doubt that I was working at the mind/body boundary. Because of the pioneering work with schizophrenia of Spotnitz (1985, 1988), Clevans (1957), Feldman (1978), Meadow (1996), Liegner (1979, 1980), and many others, modern analysts today are privileged to work on the cutting edge of the quest to reverse the schizophrenic process (Spotnitz, 1985) and other disorders considered to be biological. But the reversibility of schizophrenia remains an idea held by very few. As psychotropic drugs came into widespread use in the eighties, many psychiatrists and psychoanalysts abandoned drive theory for hermeneutical theory and left the psychoses (and other central problems) to chemical management. So, what is true and what is possible? Often what is possible resides in an accurate understanding of the problem. For this reason it seems imperative that analysts explore this new knowledge of how the brain works and submit their clinical findings to an empirical dialogue.

The new neuroscience techniques make it possible for psychoanalysis to take itself to the court of biology for corroboration or correction. A door has been opened for a dialogue between those studying the brain and psychoanalysts. We know the mind just as it emerges from brain, and neuroscientists know more and more about the brain that generates that process even though there are many controversies in this new field, such as those between the cognitive and the affective neuroscientists. Mark Solms (2002), analyst, neuropsychologist, and the primary architect of a unified brain/mind approach, neuropsychoanalysis, decries the abandonment of drive theory by many analysts and urges them to participate in the new dialogue, which will both ground the analysts' problems of subjectivity in observable biological data as well as open the complexities of the inner world that analysts know to biological consideration about how the mind works (p. 6). In May 2004, in an article in *Scientific American,* Solms wrote, "Neuroscientists are finding that their biological descriptions of the brain may fit together best when integrated by psychological theories Freud sketched a century ago" (p. 114). Eric Kandel, the 2000 Nobel Laureate in physiology, was quoted in that article, stating that psychoanalysis is "still the most coherent and intellectually satisfying view of the mind" (p. 121). This is definitely an exciting time for both fields, and a time in which they can inform one another. If we want psychoanalysis to become more efficacious, we need to make sure that it is theoretically correct, and biology can help with that. The problem of how is quite difficult because it involves discovering a methodology that can cross disciplinary lines. For example, the patient says X. We interpret it as Y, an unconscious desire for Q. But how do we know? How can we know that a piece of clinical process really is a result of this or that biological process? This paper does not pretend to answer this question; rather it is a preliminary exercise, a gathering of material from different sources as a way of beginning to look at how the two domains, brain and mind, might interact or be related.

What is Desire?

The concept of desire inspires much debate. Is it an exclusively positive concept, as popular parlance would connote, or, as some analysts point out, can it have negative aspects? "Desire," according to Webster, means "to long for, covet, express a wish for." This definition seems neither positive nor negative. That is, there isn't anything inherently positive in wishing. Is "motivation" the same thing? Webster defines it as: "any idea, need, emotion, or organic state that impels to action." That definition runs the gamut and seems to connote more about energy than desire does. But what about "covet?" That's not just wishing for something; that's wishing for something someone else has. So, desire involves both wishing and coveting. I also looked up "desire" in Rodale's (1958) *Synonym Finder* and discovered these alternatives:

1. wish for, long for, desiderate, want; yearn for, hope for, care for, pine for, sigh for; hanker after, have a yen for, covet, fancy, have a fancy for; have an eye to, be attracted to, have a mind to, have at heart, be bent upon; be inclined towards, be prone to, be predisposed towards, prefer; aspire to, emulate, set one's heart on; crave, hunger, thirst, relish; lust after, burn for, be wild or mad about, *sl.* Have the hots for, *inf.* letch after; eye, eyeball.

2. ask for, request, summon, solicit, importune; petition, entreat, urge, plead; beseech, beg, implore, supplicate, adjure; endeavor to obtain, appeal for, apply to; requisition, order, demand, require.

3. n. longing, wish, wishing, desideration, want, wanting; yearning, hope, hoping, pining, sighing, hankering, yen, itch, fondness, liking; attraction, aspiration, emulation, ambition; inclination, predilection, preference, propensity, proclivity; predisposal, predisposedness, bent, leaning, disposition; fancy, fancying, coveting, covetousness, eagerness, ardor, craving; appetency, appetite, hunger, thirst, ravenousness; relish, rapaciousness, voracity, voraciousness; avidity, greed, greediness, cupidity, avarice, graspingness; frenzy, mania, craze, rage; request, solicitation, importunity; petition, entreaty, adjuration, urge, urging; pleading, beseeching, beseechingness, begging, imploring, imploringness, imploration; supplication, prayer, appeal; application, requisition, demand, call, summons, order, requirement.

4. lust, lustfulness, concupiscence, libido, sexual appetite or urge, aphrodisiac; lewdness, bawdiness, *archaic*. Bawdry, wantonness; lasciviousness, salaciousness, salacity, lubricity, libidinousness; carnal passion, prurience, pruriency, pathol. Satyriasis, nymphomania; lechery, lecherousness, *sl.* Letch, the hots, burning; (all of animals) heat, rut, estrus; eroticism, erotism, sensuality, sexuality.

It seems that in each category of the definition there is a shift from wishing to synonyms that have more aggressive connotations, such as crave, burn, be mad about, itch, demand, covet, greed, rapaciousness, avarice, frenzy, mania, rage, demand, lust, burn, rut. So, while the very general tendency seems to be in the direction of sexual longing or urges, there is clearly a very aggressive component that enters as *the level of intensity of the desire increases*. For example, from wish for to crave or burn for; from ask for to demand; from want to greed and rage; from lust to rut. These terms almost imply that the original wish or desire begins to be impeded. Desire definitely "gets you going," definitely involves wanting something, but it is not at all clear what happens next. In order to try to clarify this further, I want to turn to Freud since psychoanalysis began with his concept of wishes.

According to Laplanche and Pontalis (1974), desire is not the same as wish in German. Lust is closer. This could be helpful as it puts desire in the sexual category and implies that wish is something different. But desire, need, demand, and wish are continually interchanged and intermingled in the literature as well as in the dictionary so it's still not clear.

Freud's conceptualization of wish, or *Wunsch*, is most clearly elucidated in the *Interpretation of Dreams* (1900), which is a reiteration of his description from the *Project* (1895). He felt that wishes refer to the experience of satisfaction "after which the mnemic image of a particular perception 'remains associated . . . with the memory-trace of the excitation produced by the need. As a result of the link that has thus been established, next time this need arises a psychical impulse will at once emerge which will seek to re-cathect the mnemic image of the perception and to re-evoke the perception itself, that is to say, to re-establish the situation of the original satisfaction. An impulse of this kind is what we call a wish; the reappearance of the perception is the fulfillment of the wish'" (in Laplanche & Pontalis, 1974, p. 482). This conceptualization of wish is a description of the way mind and body are connected. Freud here connects bodily need to psychic representation of that need and thereby explains where mind comes from. It makes sense that it is complicated. Wish and desire have taken us to the boundary between mind and body according to Freud.

Desire, Evolution, and Brain

I'd like to start thinking about the brain with a simple discussion of evolution because evolution involves the big picture about desire. Why does the turtle cross the road? Not because he's lost or because he simply enjoys a pleasant midday walk. The turtle crosses the road in order to lay an egg. It's not just a random happening. This is an ontological universe; biological creatures have a purpose. We all run on desire. According to Darwin, the purpose of every living creature is to survive and to procreate, to keep itself going. The brain has evolved over millions of years in order to serve these needs. We are always moving toward something no matter how stuck or negative we are or how hopeless we might feel. In fact, we feel hopeless because we know on some level that we are trying to go somewhere. Nature is pushing us toward fulfillment as each cell struggles to unite and communicate with others. And nature is pulling us toward death as unused or un-useful or wrecked cells stick to each other or fall away. Edward O. Wilson (1998), Harvard's preeminent sociobiologist, puts it this way: "The essential ingredient for the molding of the instincts during genetic evolution in any species [his was ants] is intelligence high enough to judge and manipulate the tension generated by the dynamism between cooperation and defection" (p. 23). (This could be looked at as another way of describing the analytic task: to help develop "intelligence high enough to judge and manipulate the tension generated by the dynamism between cooperation and defection.")

So, we are creatures with a purpose. As Spotnitz (1985) explains: Each individual has a maturational trajectory which will be completed unless there is interference from "disruptions of the maturational sequences" (p. 84), which there always are, for reasons I will discuss later.

Let's look next at Paul MacClean's triune brain (in Restak, 1979) because it is a simple image of an important concept. "In its evolution the human brain expanded in a hierarchical fashion along the lines of three basic patterns" (p. 51). These three "brains" are like three different minds. Each has its own way of perceiving and responding to the world. They constitute three behavioral domains; three different ways of experiencing time and space; three different chemistries and structures; three different "intelligences, memory systems and subjectivities" (p. 51). And the three have evolved ways of communicating with each other over the neuronal networks. Neural Darwinism teaches that connections useful for survival solidified and less adaptive ones fell away.

The old reptilian brain, consisting of the brainstem and cerebellum, is more than 100 million years old and was sufficient until the death of the last dinosaur. It is mechanical and unconscious but its basic parts are still intact and have tremendous impact on the other parts of the brain. This is the seat of what we would call instinct. Additionally, it is here that our mechanical, complex, prototypical patterns of behavior, like riding a bike or driving a car, are stored in unconscious memory. The "R complex," as MacClean calls the reptilian brain, contains at least 20 lizard behaviors concerned with self-preservation or the preservation of the species, such as the establishment of territory, growling, foraging, hoarding, greeting (display behavior), and forming groups (Restak, 1979, p. 53). Here is generated the racing heart, sweaty palms, churning stomach, and erections which we read about in our synonyms. It is here that fundamental behaviors from millions of years ago are hardwired into our current systems, and this "conservative" aspect of evolution is one of the elements that makes change difficult. For example, in this brain are the rudiments of ritualism, deception, awe for authority, pecking orders, compulsive behavior, and imitation (p. 53). Archetypal patterns are set here, waiting for a stimulus to rouse them. For example, a lizard in a zoo pays no attention to anything until a shadowgram of a lizard is put before him (p. 55). He then walks over and gives a full lizard display. Display behavior, opening the thighs and showing an erect genital, is an innate characteristic, shown immediately after birth. In spite of its obvious sexual overtones, its purpose, according to MacClean and others, is to establish dominance rather than initiate sex.

Dominance, power, survival—but we're supposed to be discussing human desire. Look around. Who's dominant? How is the authority perceived? Is there any awe in your life? What pecking order are you in? Do you like your place? Can you move out of it? Who are you sharing a house with? Are you dominant or submissive? Have you done any growling? Is this dominance or sex? Have you displayed any new clothes recently? One can ask similar questions about a narcissistic transference where we're taught to ask ourselves what kind of relationship the patient wants with us. Does he growl or is he mute? How ritualistic are the sessions? How does the patient respond to any changes in the pattern? Does he seem rigid or flexible? Is he pleased with your attempt to be "like" him? When you think of repetitive patterns and the difficulty of change in psychoanalysis, think of the old reptilian brain.

As mammals emerged, the limbic system was the next brain area to develop and is often referred to as the old mammalian brain. The thalamus allowed sight, smell, and hearing to operate together; the amygdala and hippocampus created a crude memory system (we began to remember what scared us instead of depending only on perception); and the hypothalamus enabled the organism to react to more stimuli. Emotions are generated here but are not experienced, do not become conscious, here. The limbic system surrounds the brainstem but also makes connections with the newer, greatly expanded cerebral cortex. An enormous amount of recent brain research centers on the limbic system and the role of emotion in consciousness. Think of the limbic system as a wheel with the cortex a huge tire surrounding it says Restak (1979, p. 60). The wheel contains hormones, drives, and temperature control and reward-and-punishment centers as well as the memory system in the hippocampus. This is the center for the four Fs: feeding, fighting, fleeing, and fucking. MacLean thinks that the limbic system is nature's way of giving the reptilian brain a thinking cap, to help emancipate it from stereotypical behavior that was no longer adaptive (in Restak, p. 57). Similarly the greatly expanded cerebral cortex, the "third" brain, evolved with the advent of language in order to free us further for adaptive choices. But, I'm more interested in the two "lower" brains; the neuronal connections from these bottom brains upward are a great deal stronger than those from the cortex downward. That's why it's so difficult to change your feeling via reason, and why a strong feeling can wipe out any brilliant thought you might be having.

So, one could think of a psychoanalysis as a recapitulation of the evolutionary project: to give the individual enough cortical intelligence to free him, to as great an extent as possible, from the repetitive, stereotypical behavior these two brains insist on. But I'm getting ahead of myself. I still haven't come to any conclusions about the biology of desire.

Affective Neuroscience and the Rudiments of Desire

Within the field of neuroscience, there is a huge divide between the cognitive neuroscientists and the affective neuroscientists. It is somewhat similar to the divide in psychoanalysis between those who consider it an hermeneutical discipline and those who consider it a natural science complete with biological causation. The cognitive researchers represent a continuation of the behaviorist tradition in psychology—the idea that words and environmental events are sufficient to explain behavior. They represent by far the strongest position in terms of numbers and influence. For them, affect is secondary, a byproduct of thought. Of the affective neuroscientists, by far the most influential is Jaak Panksepp, who has spent his career doing research on rats and cats, meticulously discovering and documenting the emotional systems in the brain and their interaction with the brainstem and neocortex. His work describes the primacy of affect, which is older than thought. Again, the issue of truth is at stake: Which group is right? And again there is a lack of dialogue between the two groups. One group says affect is primary; a second says it is secondary. Upon these assertions entire edifices of clinical and social theory are built. But which is true? How can these theories be tested?

Rudiments of Desire: Emotional Systems in the Brain

For the purposes of this paper, which has been exploring the evolutionary basis of psychoanalysis, the Panksepp findings about the roots of emotion will be explicated because there has been a great deal of empirical work in this area and because these concepts are remarkably compatible with modern psychoanalysis. Keep in mind, however, that we are comparing animal studies with human phenomena. Even though a good argument can be made for doing this, it must be emphasized that it is just a way of comparing a theory from one discipline with findings from another and it does not "prove" anything.

It's important for our discussion of desire to understand how these emotional systems work. The mechanism is counterintuitive. We are used to thinking that emotions are "caused" by events (the conscious experience). We see a bear and become afraid and run. Something bad happens to us, and we feel sad. This is common sense. This is the position of the cognitive neuroscientists: emotion is just a subdivision of declarative thought. Panksepp (1998), like William James 100 years ago, disagrees. We are afraid because we run. We are sad because something activated our sad system. We can be sad without knowing what happened. Circuitry for the emotions is hardwired, ready to be activated by an internal or external stimulus (p. 49).

Panksepp's discoveries provide so much ostensible corroboration for psychoanalytic drive theory that I will mention just a few of his findings before returning to the questions about desire.

1. "Feelings are not simply mental events; rather they arise from neurobiological events . . . emotional states arise from material events that mediate and modulate the deep instinctual nature of many human and animal action tendencies. One reason such instinctual states may include an internally experienced feeling tone is that higher organisms possess neurally based self-representation systems" (Panksepp, 1998, p. 58). In other words, it's one thing to be impelled into action by a feeling; it's another to "feel" a feeling. As humans, we experience both. Analysts often have the experience of a feeling "in the room" that the patient seems to be completely unaware of. Something is necessary for feelings to be "felt" but that doesn't mean that they don't exist. Is it our job, as analysts, to help create enough mind for the unfelt feelings to be felt?

2. The fact that the emotional circuits are in the limbic system, which is millions of years old, rather than in the cortex, which is only 100,000 years old, implies that there were emotional systems long before there was mind with which to interpret them. Was there then affect before consciousness? It would seem so.

3. Nature gives us the ability to feel and behave in certain ways, and learning allows us to effectively use those systems to navigate the complexities of the world. When we say, "This or that behavior is inherited," what we should be saying is that "certain psycho-behavioral tendencies can be represented within the intrinsic brain and body constructions that organisms inherit" (Panksepp, 1998, p. 16). "No specific thoughts or behaviors are directly inherited, but *dispositions* to feel, think, and act in various ways and in various situations are. Although these tendencies do not necessarily dictate our destinies,

they powerfully promote certain possibilities and diminish others" (Panksepp, 1998, p. 16). While basic emotional circuits are among the tools provided by nature, their ability to permanently change the life course and personalities of organisms depends on the nurturance or lack of nurturance that the world provides. Everything is epigenetic, a mix of nature and nurture.

4. Maintaining the plasticity of the brain is comparable to exercising the body: "Emotional systems can surely be strengthened by use and weakened by disuse" (Panksepp, 1998, p. 17).

5. Emotional systems can be activated independently of the environment. This accounts for free-floating feeling and is evidence of the genetic nature of the emotional circuits. Think of how valuable these emotional systems would be to the lizard. Finally he could make some choices on the basis of what felt good and what didn't or what aroused anger or panic. His ability to get goods and survive and to develop social systems would increase tremendously.

6. Emotional circuits are "genetically predetermined to respond unconditionally to stimuli arising from major life-challenging circumstances" (Panksepp, 1998, p. 48). While the systems were designed to respond to real-world events, they are not constructed from those events but represent the ability of certain types of stimuli to access the neural circuitry. We are afraid because we run. We're roused to act to save ourselves and then, eventually, the feeling of fear trickles up through the cortical language system. Emotion is an *effect*. Feelings are the effects of arousal systems in the brain. They are not causes. Something arouses the circuitry; later, the cortex explains what it was. The fact that these emotional potentials exist within the neural circuits of the brain independently of external influences makes it possible for unregulated and excessive activities within these systems to contribute to major psychiatric disorders. Psychoanalysts are regulators of these primary emotional systems. Some need liberating, and some need calming down.

Desire in Biological Terms

Panksepp (1998) outlines four primary emotional circuits in the mammalian brain: rage, fear, panic, seeking. It's interesting that three of the four systems relate to dealing with danger of some kind and only one to going out and getting things. This is perhaps another reason why change is so difficult: we are always on the defensive. In introducing the "seeking system," Panksepp (1998) states:

> The desires and aspirations of the human heart are endless. It is foolish to attribute them all to a single brain system. But they all come to a standstill if certain brain systems, such as the dopamine (DA) circuits arising from midbrain nuclei, are destroyed. (p. 144)

These circuits seem to account for feelings of engagement and excitement as we "seek material resources" needed for bodily survival. Without them, "human aspirations remain frozen in an endless winter of discontent" (Panksepp, 1998, p. 144). If these dopamine synapses are active, anything is possible. Panksepp thinks that excessive firing of synapses here may account for mania and hallucinations. That is, overactivity in this seeking system pushes our imagination beyond the bounds of reality (p. 145). I'm reminded of descriptions of anhedonia (the inability to experience pleasure) and concomitant hopelessness in schizophrenia, of a schizophrenic patient, now hopeless, who began treatment in a state of extreme paranoid excitement.

"The mammalian brain," Panksepp (1998) explains, "contains a 'foraging/exploration/investigation/curiosity/interest/expectancy/SEEK-ING' system that . . . has a characteristic feeling tone . . . akin to that invigorated feeling of anticipation we experience when we actively seek thrills and other rewards" (p. 145). This system responds to homeostatic imbalances and environmental incentives. A rat will self-stimulate this system until exhaustion if given a chance. He is not pressing a lever for a reward; he is trying to *get something* behind the lever. This is an appetitive motivational system that mediates "wanting" as opposed to "liking" (p. 145). Panksepp thinks that this system, when connecting to cortical processes in humans, accounts for the search for meaning and causality. But where is the reinforcement in this system? asks Panksepp. It was tempting to assume that the reward for the behavior is some "pleasure" in consuming. But on the contrary, ". . . the pleasures and reinforcements of consummatory processes appear to be more closely linked to a *reduction of arousal* in this brain system" (p. 147, italics added). The pleasure is in the tension reduction in the seeking system. The excitement is in the search, and the reward is in the reduction of tension. The object procured or consumed does not matter. A "goad without a goal" is how Panksepp puts it (p. 144). So, it seems that desire, biologically speaking—unsophisticated desire in the most ancient emotional system—is open-ended. In the process of trying to track down the biology of desire, we may have stumbled upon a biological corroboration of drive theory.

Desire and Sex

It's true that sex is one of the things that we "desire" to go after. Even the lizards had sex. But, interestingly enough, Panksepp doesn't claim to know much about the affective elements of the sexual instinct. He knows that we all do it, but he doesn't know much about how it *feels*. There is also a large unknown area between sex and "nurturing." MacClean (in Restak, 1979) said that the only thing humans do that lizards don't do is "altruistic behavior and . . . parental behavior" (p. 53). Apparently no one knows how nurturing behavior evolved from non-nurturing behavior. All we know is that when it happened, it produced an enormous change in the brain. Nurturant circuits are closely connected with sexual circuits, but they are different. Lizards have sex but don't nurture. In males the circuits of sexuality and aggression are very close together. Men have erections when going into battle, which helps explain rape during war. Much more is known about what happens during male orgasm than what occurs during female orgasm. Apparently female orgasm was less necessary for the preservation of the species than was male orgasm. Vasopressin is the hormone that is released during male arousal. It also makes men jealously attack interlopers. Oxytocin is the hormone that women experience during orgasm, and it is also released during lactation. "During the last days of pregnancy and the first few days of lactation, there are remarkable increases in oxytocin receptors in several brain areas. . . . During lactation, oxytocin cells begin to communicate with each other directly via the development of *gap junctions* between adjacent oxytocinergic neurons, allowing them to synchronize their neural messages precisely. This helps suckling stimuli from nursing babies to more effectively trigger oxytocin secretion in the brain of the mother, presumably to sustain a maternal mood" (Panksepp, 1998, p. 251). In other words, women are wired to allow babies to "turn on" their mothering feelings. But even with the help of hormones, maternal behavior is sketchy; some are good at it, and some are not so good. It seems to be a fragile connection in spite of the momentous consequences. There is very little actual research on the relationship between maternal behavior and social bonding. And, according to Panksepp, there is practically no way of studying how these feelings (friendships, family attachments, and romantic relationships) might be constructed from specific brain activities (p. 249). Others discuss how the interactions between caretaker and child during the first 18 months of life determine how the neurons are patterned. More popular writers talk about how early experiences are registered emotionally in the limbic system and say that in the cortex we can loosen the grip of these early emotional experiences. For example, according to Pally (2000), "Maturation of the cortex via verbalization can take advantage of cortical plasticity to modulate deeply engrained emotional responses" (p. 88).

Now I'd like to re-examine Freud's conceptualization of wish, discussed earlier in the paper. But before we do this, a brief consideration of the way in which the brain constructs perceptions will be helpful. Our brain does not simply register the environment the way a camera does. On the contrary, the brain detects individual stimulus features of the environment (environment here can mean internal imagery as well as external), such as edges, contours, line orientation, color, form, pitch, volume, and movement, and then processes them in separate regions of the cortex. It then "takes the pattern of neuronal activity created by the simultaneous processing of all these individual environmental features, and compares it with patterns stored in memory" (Pally, 2000, p. 19). Different neuronal colonies have different processing preferences: some like line and motion; others prefer social cues. When a match for the current pattern is found, perception occurs. Motivation, emotion, and memory all affect these choices.

Back to Freud

Freud (in Laplanche & Pontalis, 1974) said the experience of satisfaction, for example, from a good feed, "creates a mnemic image of a particular perception" (I'm guessing that this is facilitated by oxytocin) which "remains associated with the memory trace of the excitation produced by the need" (p. 482). I think we can now deconstruct what this means. A good feed reduces the tension aroused by hunger and results in a pleasurable sensation. This pleasurable sensation connects with the memory of the state of arousal. A link has been established between the state of arousal and the perception of satisfaction. The need is the wish. The perception is of the fulfillment of the wish. They are linked in memory thanks to oxytocin. Or, to put it differently, the feeling of wanting, the excitement of going out to search, which can be conscious, connects with a *perception* of satisfaction. Every arousal now evokes this perception (or symbol) of satisfaction. A bodily event has become symbolized because it provided the satisfaction of tension reduction. The search for objects in the real world is entirely governed by this relationship with symbols. They make up the unconscious fantasies that govern our search. Desire driven by archaic images keeps us chasing rainbows. The current object only matters to the extent that it triggers these imagos.

Conclusions and Speculations

Freud's concept of wish is at the heart of psychoanalysis. It explains how we develop the mental equipment with which to carry on the evolutionary struggle. Wishes begin with instinctual needs in the oldest area of the brain. Then the seeking system is aroused to go out and find something. The experience of tension reduction makes the search pleasurable. Although desire and wish are often used interchangeably, technically speaking desire is closer to lust and the fundamental urge for sex and union. And, it is procreation that keeps everything going. But in order to pursue our desire, we also need to satisfy our basic needs for food, water, warmth, dominance, etc. If things were simple, our minds would enable us to imagine endless ways of satisfying these needs, endless kinds of hunger-tension reduction, endless kinds of sex-tension reduction. But because our world is fraught with dangers, other emotional systems have evolved which can easily be aroused and interfere with our satisfying desire. Panksepp (1998) mentions three: fear (flight behaviors), rage (fight/biting and attacking), and panic (in mammals, distress over attachment) (p. 53). In the animal world, interference with desire results in action of some kind. But in the human world, because of the development of language whereby dangers can be symbolized, civilization, and the cerebral cortex, interfere with desire, resulting in defenses and repetitions. If the individual does not know or cannot obtain what he or she wants, he/she gets stuck in unproductive "neuronal pathways." And so it is up to the analyst to intervene indirectly to resolve these blocks (Spotnitz, 1985, p. 87).

Liberating Desire: A Case Example

Young, beautiful, bright, articulate, and cooperative, this patient entered treatment because she wanted to get married and have children.

At first she became involved with an extremely mean, difficult, and withholding man, but eventually she extricated herself from that relationship. She then had an affair with a man she liked a lot. But he began to reject her. She left him for another man who was much more responsive to her. But she couldn't get the previous man out of her head. In a recent session, she said:

> It's Henry again. I think of him constantly. I've never experienced anything like this. It makes no sense. I want this guy who doesn't want me—he can't stand my wanting anything from him. He says he wants a wife and children but his best buddy is gay. I found gay porn web sites on his computer. He only wants to see me in a group, or when I'm down and out. Why do I want him?
>
> He reminds me of my mother. He's moody. You can never tell what mood he'll be in. I had to get over wanting my mother. I learned that nothing she did was predictable from my behavior. Well, I really didn't give her up—I still have the longing. Now it's for Henry. I need to move it onto someone who would give me more of what I want, or you, but I can't seem to do it.

Although this woman has a structured mind, it is organized in such a way that she goes after what she consciously says she does not want. She is stuck in an emotional rut, cathected to the feeling of distance, unpredictability, unwantedness. A whole cluster of negative emotions is tied to her image of an object. When she thinks of wanting, she conjures up this kind of experience. What does she need in order to be liberated?

Let's consider what she is telling us from a psycho-biological perspective. At a cortical level she seems to be saying, "Oh, please, send me a prince, and I will live happily ever after." But the old reptilian brain, at a lower level, is saying, "No, no, a thousand times no! I will not budge." And, in the middle, the emotional configuration (let's imagine it's a combination of wanting and "can't having") is producing feelings of endless suffering. So what should I do? I assume that she needs to verbalize things she's never said and to have feelings she's not had. Then she'll have enough cortical control to be able to move to a better object/imago. To do this, I must first of all deal with the old reptilian self, the self that doesn't want to change no matter what. I have to join her and imitate her so she won't be roused to fight me. "Well, for now you want Henry. So what if we work on getting him?" But I also have to remember the emotional "self" and how she needs a new and better experience with me, little by little, mouthfuls of milk. I'll provide this experience by joining her wherever she goes, assuring a state of acceptance so she can make the decision to move or not to move. This speaks to the limbic connection with the old reptilian brain; these two stubborn "brains" will only move under their own steam. I'll also want to join her when I work with her conscious desires, emanating from the cortex. Spotnitz (1997) recommends that we "Gratify any reasonable request. See if they improve." This will help her know her wishes and develop new ones. She'll become able to shift her search to one more pleasurable. All of these techniques help to give the patient a different experience, and as this happens, she will become able to say new things and forge new choices in new pathways. Her desire to repeat a negative emotional experience will loosen, and she will develop an ability to tolerate the fruits of a positive desire.

REFERENCES

Carter, R. (1998), *Mapping the Mind*. London: Orion Books.
Clevans, E. (1957), the fear of a schizophrenic man. *Psychoanalysis,* 5 (4):58–67.
Feldman, Y. (1978), The early history of modern psychoanalysis. *Modern Psychoanalysis,* 3:15–27.
Freud, S. (1895), Project for a scientific psychology. *Standard Edition.* London: Hogarth Press, 1:283–397.
———— (1900), Interpretation of dreams. *Standard Edition.* London: Hogarth Press, 4 & 5.
Laplanche, J. & J. Pontalis (1974), *The Language of Psychoanalysis.* Donald Nicholson-Smith, translator. New York: W.W. Norton.
Liegner, E. (1979), Solving a problem in a case of psychosis. *Modern Psychoanalysis,* 4:5–17.
———— (1980, The hate that cures: the psychological reversibility of schizophrenia. *Modern Psychoanalysis* 5:5–95.
Meadow, P. (1996), The selected theoretical and clinical papers. *Modern Psychoanalysis* 21(2).
Pally, R. (2000), *The Mind-Brain Relationship.* London and New York: Karnac Books.
Panksepp, J. (1998), *Affective Neuroscience.* New York and London: Oxford University Press.
Restak, R. (1979), *The Brain: The Last Frontier.* New York: Doubleday.
Rodale, J. I. (1958), *The Synonym Finder.* New York: Rodale Books.
Solms, M. (2002), *The Brain and the Inner World.* New York: Other Press.
———— (2004), Freud returns. *Scientific American,* May.

Spotnitz, H. (1985), *Modern Psychoanalysis of the Schizophrenic Patient.* Second Edition. New York: Human Sciences Press.
——— (1997), Personal communication.
Wilson, E. (1998), The biological basis of morality. *The Atlantic Monthly,* April.

36 Hawthorn Street
Cambridge, MA 02138
maryshepherd@comcast.net

Modern Psychoanalysis
Vol. XXX, No. 1, 2005

Listening With the Intuitive Ear

THEODORE LAQUERCIA

This paper considers intuitive processes as they relate to how analysts listen to patients and how intuition may inform some of our emotional communication interventions. It suggests that we train ourselves and our students and supervisees to be attuned to unconscious communications that emanate from all strata of cortical areas including the most primitive. Case vignettes drawn from clinical practice and classroom presentations that describe interventions formed by intuition or unknown experience are presented and offer a way to understand such experience as a means to resonate with the patients we treat.

If, as analysts, we are to understand the primitive motivations that emanate from the unconscious processes of our patients, we must train ourselves to listen to the deepest levels of their communications. This is why, I believe, we must grapple with the role that intuition plays in our interactions with our patients as we develop our theories and techniques. For purposes of this paper, "intuition" is defined as: "The immediate apprehension of an object [or idea] by the mind without the intervention of any reasoning process" (*Oxford,* 1973). And if, in the course of the analytic hour, we strive to engage in all levels of experience with our patients, then the deepest, primordial aspects of our being must also be engaged. How we process these rudimentary communications, how we learn to use them, and how we might be able to train others to use their own intuitive powers will be the focus of this paper. Recent findings from the field of neuroscience will also inform my argument.

In the treatment room, the analyst sits in a special silence. As he listens to his patients, he becomes aroused with thoughts, feelings, and ideas and assigns meaning to the unfolding narrative from his own theoretical perspective. This theoretical operating frame, neuroscientists tell us, resides within the neocortex, the topmost stratum of the cerebral cortex, the area of the brain responsible for higher level thinking; the techniques that flow from it are arrived at in a systematic way. And yet, analytic experience is neither logical nor systematic. In fact, the multiplicity of emotions that the analyst feels within himself and within his relationship with the patient are, I believe, much more complex than the explanatory power of any single theory. A dynamic interrelatedness ebbs and flows from all levels of cortical functioning in both analyst and patient. In that special analytic silence, questions often arise in the practitioner's mind about what is being said, what is not being said, and what is being obfuscated by the patient's varied and intricate language. Within this frame, the analyst's interventions are subject to an array of internal experiences that engage both conscious and unconscious processes. This interaction is an often barely decipherable nexus, one that may create a conundrum for the analyst. He may wonder, "How much of what is perceived is emanating from my psyche and how much is emanating from the psyche of the patient?"

The literature is filled with references to interventions that suggest the use of intuitive processes, (Reik, 1948; Lomas, 1993; Meadow, 2003), but critics of psychoanalysis argue that the validity of the psychoanalytic process is called into question by the unreliability of these interventions. This paper is an attempt to respond to that criticism.

In order to understand the difficulty of explicating the role of intuition within the clinical relationship, we must reiterate that it is higher-level reasoning that leads to interpretation and that this thinking process is continuously at work in our efforts to assign meaning to patients' communications. This attempt at deriving meaning is an intellectual effort. This linear and logical way of thinking resides within the left hemisphere of the brain, the area where speech and language are developed, although the right hemisphere, where creativity and intuition reside, must also be engaged in a process that incorporates both abstraction and feeling. This coordination makes these two spheres partners in our attempts to decipher a patient's words. However, there is a second substratum of the brain, the limbic system, a deeply embedded primitive center where memory and feeling reside, that must also be taken into account when formulating interventions. The amygdala, part of the limbic system, whose function is to help us distinguish perceptions that signal danger, also plays an important role when we are faced with intuitive responses to fear. I believe that when a patient lies on the couch and experiences feelings of vulnerability, his perceptions are heightened because these primitive brain centers are aroused and receptive. Hence communications that speak to these deepest areas in an emotional way are what analysts should strive for. A true connection is made when the primitive unconscious processes of both analyst and patient are in tune.

Meadow (1991) uses the term "resonance" to describe communications derived from those deep levels of experience where drives are felt, suppressed, repressed, or denied. Sheftel (1998) cites instances of nonverbal communications used by analysts in order to understand patients' process, and Laquercia (1998) writes about communications transmitted symbolically that appear on the surface inexplicable to ordinary logical understanding. Bollas (1992) refers to this resonant mode of communication as the "unknown thought." This receptive way of listening is meant to bridge the gap between the complexity of the patient's primitive, nonverbal, affective experience and the speech and abstraction that emanate from his ability for higher-level cognitive functioning (Lewis, Amini & Lannon, 2001). As the patient uses language to describe what he thinks about who he is and how he got that way, he emotes, to a degree, but primarily he is telling the analyst what he thinks. However, the analyst must keep in mind that this communication is, in fact, a higher order translation of memory and feeling. To understand the totality of what is being expressed, we must look beyond the patient's words to the disguised yet charged emotional content of the denied, unremembered, or never experienced. Lewis, Amini and Lannon (2001) remind us that it is the more primitive part of the brain that controls feeling. It is this archaic residue that makes analytic work so complex: "Words, good ideas, and logic mean nothing to at least two brains out of three. Much of one's mind does not take orders. . . . It is apparent that the entire neocortex of humans continues to be regulated by the paralimbic regions from which it evolved" (p. 33).

As clinicians, we sit in our analytic silence with all of our perceptual potential engaged and are inclined to use the evolved cortical system to do the work of understanding while we struggle simultaneously with arousals from the primitive limbic system. Logic and reason press for accommodation when we listen to patient process, yet we know there is more to be understood. Language is a double-edged sword. It can foster communication, and yet it can also limit our experience of what the patient is conveying. Early preverbal experiences are dominated and shaped by the deeper regions of the brain, organized originally and primarily to ensure survival.

Framing this argument in developmental terms, we are of course reminded that an infant exists in a realm of feeling and lacks the ability to rationally decipher the world around him but, instead, "senses" and intuits experiences of satisfaction and dissatisfaction. But as higher functioning develops, he resorts less and less to purely instinctual modes of communicating and begins to use the newly acquired power of language to reason and to get his needs met. And yet those early experiences of pleasure and unpleasure remain encoded in the brain and continue to influence feelings and actions. From a psychoanalytic perspective, helping patients express these primitive sensations in language remains our most difficult task. Lewis, Amini and Lannon (2001) frame this dilemma in the language of neuroscience: The "limbic brain . . . can move us in ways beyond logic that have only the most inexact translations in a language that the neocortex can comprehend" (p. 34). Our patients, therefore have to struggle with verbal expression in an attempt to maintain a logical sense while underlying feelings compete to reveal deeper meaning. This at times results in communication befuddled by these conflicting forces.

Clinical Vignettes

Three recent clinical vignettes illustrate these conflicting modes of communication. In the first case, Mr. B, who in the midst of telling me about an ordinary workplace situation in which a subordinate was causing managerial problems, suddenly exclaimed, "Why am I telling you all this? . . . Why do I even bother?" His tone was one of irritation, and like many times before in session, this kind of remark led to a stubborn silence and a sense of exasperation. I intervened by asking him, "What happens when you say that? Are you feeling something? . . . Is there some feeling that triggers that kind of comment?" Agitated, he replied,

> It reminds me of when I was in the fifth grade with Mrs. Shapiro. . . . Everything feels like that. The air in here feels like it. . . . The lighting is like the way it was in that school. That Mrs. Shapiro was such a bitch! I was so afraid. She'd say, "That's the wrong thing. Just shut up and pay attention." She was so scary. They didn't hit you in that school, but it was as if it would happen. The anger was really severe. Even the smell of certain kinds of perfume makes me have that feeling. I react from sensing these things. The way the air feels in here, the lighting . . . all of it makes me feel that old way. It's hard to get over that fear. I feel scared.

Mr. Z, the second patient, often complained that when he gets angry he has trouble finding the "perfect words" to describe what he is experiencing and feeling. This difficulty speaks to the conflict he feels when he tries to use his intellectual abilities to put his feelings into the "straightjacket" of verbal expression. He sputters and feels embarrassed by his incoherence. He places all of his effort into intellectual expression and clings to the misguided hope that he can explain his feeling through his thought processes. It has become apparent to me over time, however, that he uses every bit of his energy to avoid feelings and that he instead uses his superior intellect to dampen the emotional expression of his life experience. His search for the perfect words moves him away from the feeling that has motivated that search. The consequence of this stultified communication is that others react to him in ways he cannot comprehend.

Mr. T, the third patient, while in the midst of describing an interaction with his estranged wife, who had damaged a valuable object that belonged to him, found that he could not recall the details of the exchange, saying, "I can't remember the words or details of the experience because, when I get mad like that, I get confused and words elude me." His arousal to an unacceptable feeling state put him in a state of confusion; his reasoning capacities and his ability to remember fell victim to his anger.

Discussion

In the case of Mr. B, who seemingly was simply reporting on a current work situation in which problems with a subordinate aroused feelings of fright in him, it was only after he was able to describe the olfactory sensations and memories of the hated teacher and classroom that I was able to decipher the "deeper" hidden source of his fear. This clinical example illustrates that a fear of survival takes precedence over everything else in our perceptual system. All of our senses are utilized to keep us safe and are poised to pick up cues that signal danger or precipitants to unacceptable action. These mechanisms are not often in our conscious awareness, but nonetheless rule our behavior. In this session Mr. B described perceptions not understood intellectually by the analyst yet experienced so deeply by the patient that they led to a memory of a repetitive, visceral response to perceived danger. These memories, as we have seen, were of a threatening authority figure and reveal the unconscious strategies he uses when he feels afraid.

As this vignette reveals, multiple perceptual events occur in the course of a session that are often outside of our conscious awareness and that come into focus only when they are called to our attention or when they reach a threshold of experience that can be put into words. When Mr. B moved into an agitated silence, I intervened, and the patient was finally able to express verbally the sensory cues underlying his fear. Fear is a chronic state for him, embedded in his mental life and unconsciously connected to the "in vivo" moment experienced in my office. By connecting the perceptual cues aroused in my presence to a memory, he was finally able to make sense of his feeling of futility in the face of perceived danger. This ability to match present with past is a function of how memory is stored. Feeling and thought, memory and association are compressed and have the potential for release in the course of an interaction with the analyst. However, when the analyst confronts material that on the surface may appear bizarre and even, at times, psychotic, this material becomes intelligible only upon closer examination. Intuitive responses, I believe, present us with opportunities to craft interventions that advance our understanding of psychotic processes.

The Role of Intuition in the Treatment of Psychosis

When confronted with the language of psychosis and the difficulty in making sense of psychotic productions, our intuitive perceptions should be welcomed and appreciated. In the example just presented, the analyst struggles to assign meaning to words that appear to have no meaning and that arouse anxiety and confusion. And yet this schizophrenic patient is attempting to do what all patients do, convey to the analyst a puzzling internal experience. And, if the analyst is listening and engaged in intuitive processing, he will be able to derive a better understanding of what the patient is struggling to convey. When receptive to his intuition, the analyst may use his feelings to intervene and, in doing so, may resolve some of the confusion in his mind. Some theorists call this use of the analyst's feeling drawing upon one's own objective countertransference reactions (Spotnitz, 2004) and others call it projective identification (Ogden, 1982).

An excellent example of an intuitive response was reported in a case treated by a classically trained analyst (Szalita-Pemov, 1955) working in a hospital setting. She describes the experience in this way: "Four years ago I began work with a very sick schizophrenic woman who had been hospitalized for some thirteen years. . . . She was assaultive and neglectful of her appearance. She walked around nude and defecated on the floor and on plates when food was served to her. She was kept in seclusion most of the time" (p. 13). Clinically trained to explore and reflect questions and to remain silent until an interpretation was warranted, this analyst was at a loss as to how to respond when confronted by a flow of nearly unintelligible statements by this regressed woman. When the patient barraged her with personal questions, the analyst wondered if she should maintain her "analytic" stance or respond to her in a new way. And when, sensing from her accent that she was French, the patient asked her, "Is Rue des Capucines all right to live in?" she was still undecided as to the best course to take.

> I meditated: Should I be analytical and turn the question back to her, or should I answer the question? I favored the latter. A picture of the street she had mentioned came to my mind. I was not sure, however, that I had the right street in mind, so I answered rather hesitantly, "It is a somewhat noisy street, but it is quite all right to live in." "This is exactly what I felt about it," she responded rather cheerfully. "My brother was of a different opinion." Whereupon the patient . . . wrapped herself more carefully, straightened her posture, and mumbl[ed], "I'd better be nice to this nice little lady." This marked a change in the behavior of the patient and the session continued with the patient and the analyst sharing exchanges about their experiences in Europe during the Second World War. (p. 14)

I believe that by abandoning, at least temporarily, the traditional analytic stance of only reflecting questions, this clinician responded *intuitively* and was rewarded by a patient who suddenly appeared more intact and more able to begin the process of establishing a relationship with the "nice little lady."

Clinical Vignettes

An example from my own practice of an unexpected but successful intuitive response reveals a similar dynamic. As a patient complained about the unnecessary formality of addressing each other by our last names, claiming she had always been just Laura, I asked why she didn't use her husband's last name. When she reacted as though I were making a recommendation that she do so, I explained to her that the purpose of my question was simply to understand. She eventually responded that her husband's name was too ethnic sounding and added that she didn't like hers either, but "it's what it is." I then intuitively asked, "How about using Laquercia?" Pleased, she said that would be nice and repeated over and over, "Laura Laquercia," and added that it had a nice alliterative sound to it, a kind of fluid alliteration. But still unsatisfied, she continued to want to know why I couldn't simply call her Laura.

It then became clear to me that the issue was not whether she would use her husband's name or mine, but rather whether she would be successful in influencing my behavior toward her. As the session drew to an end, I decided to call her Laura. Initially, there was silence, but when she responded, her tone was filled with a level of emotion absent earlier in the session. She said that she felt very moved by my use of her first name and that she had always felt powerless to affect me in any way and to get what she wanted from me. I became convinced that her veiled complaint at the beginning, and again during the session, warranted a response from me that, intuitively, was risky yet yielded a deeper level of communication. She then was able to express, vividly, feelings about me and our relationship and the futility of her attempts to influence me. Calling her Laura had made her feel that she could exert some influence over me after all. In the remaining session time, she told me that she had experienced new feelings for me during the previous week. And although she thought of me as attractive, she said she had never felt sexually aroused by me. This week she had.

Another clinical example involves a supervisee who suffered from a series of medical disturbances and who was seeking intervention from his doctors. As they attempted to relieve his many symptoms, it became clear that they were also responding to his emotional distress; in addition to prescribing medicine to cure his ailments, they also prescribed mild psychotropic drugs and sleeping pills. Since I had known him for a long time, I was familiar with his pattern of taking on more duties than he could comfortably handle; these included a busy New York practice, teaching, lecturing, writing, and testing responsibilities as well as agency evaluations. In a session dominated by talk of physical distress, he finally erupted into a tirade of psychotic proportion. Intervening intuitively, I told him that he was a glutton with too much on his plate. At that moment, I was struck by a mental image of an insatiable man at a banquet feast devouring food from an overflowing plate. He was gorging himself with more professional food than he could digest, food that often didn't agree with him. I said, "If you keep this up, you'll be in a wheelchair licking an ice cream cone with your tongue dangling from one side of your mouth like a stroke victim." In the following session he reported that his condition had improved considerably and that he had discontinued the use of the psychotropic drugs and sleeping aids. Even his digestive distress had abated. He also told me that the two interventions I had made in the previous session had had a great impact on him. He laughed as he recalled my description of him in a wheelchair licking an ice cream cone and conceded that I had been correct in my assessment that he had too much on his plate and that his gluttony had probably contributed greatly to his gastric distress. He then announced that he had reduced his professional activities to be more in line with an appropriate "diet" of responsibilities. My intuitive intervention had helped him to examine more closely the relationship between his physical condition and his professional life.

Training Students to Use Intuition

Despite its apparent importance in clinical practice, modern psychoanalytic theorists have written little about the role of intuition in crafting interventions. And although Spotnitz and Meadow (1976) agree that intuition is one of the most important attributesy that a psychoanalytic candidate exhibit when being considered for admission for training, our literature does not reflect this belief. The three areas that have been consistently felt to be a necessary part of institute training, a personal analysis, coursework, and supervision, have all received a lot of attention in the literature because they are presumed to adequately prepare candidates to recognize inductions, arousals, and countertransference reactions. However, investigations of the subtle, often inexplicable, shifts in perception emanating from the depths of the psyche that often guide analysts' responses rarely appear in the literature. And yet it is these unexpected and emotionally charged responses that frequently yield the most dramatic clinical results.

Although Meadow (2003) and Lomas (1993) have both stated that analytic candidates should be helped to develop their intuitive powers, no one has yet devised a way of systematically accomplishing this goal. Since intuition is an "instinctive" process utilized to a degree by everyone, I recommend that an investigation of its sources and curative potential be incorporated into class experience and the supervisory process.

Often, when an individual senses that a feeling is not immediately intelligible, there is a tendency to deny or refute it as unimportant, insignificant, or even crazy. But, in fact, it is in training seminars and in supervision that intuitive responsiveness can be developed and nurtured. Students should be helped to trust and to use their intuition in the same environment of safety we strive to provide for our patients. The stance that the analyst takes with a patient, that of being a nonjudgmental "safe object" to whom the patient can say everything, should be replicated in the supervisory process. Thus, when a student reports that an intervention was "wrong," an investigation of the origins of this "wrong" response might yield some interesting results. I have found that focusing on a purely cognitive understanding of the experience, rather than on the psychodynamic relationship in the room, often distances us from a student's intuitive understanding of a dynamic in favor of a more logical explanation. This intellectual pursuit neglects to take into account the as yet unknown cause of the "mistaken" intuitive intervention. Sometimes these so-called mistakes reveal a great deal about the candidate's ability to "listen" to the patient, an ability that should be celebrated and not discarded in favor of a more intellectual deconstruction of patient history or verbal reports.

In "Trends in Modern Psychoanalytic Supervision," Spotnitz (1976) recommends that the attitude of a supervisor toward a supervisee should replicate that of an analyst toward a patient. A supervisor should help the candidate say everything he can about his clinical work without criticism or intervention that would lead him to believe that he is being evaluated. This attitude maximizes the student's potential to develop his intuitive senses. Spotnitz further reminds us that "[a]ny intuitive understanding the student [analyst] may have is usually deeply repressed, so that he feels far removed from the patient" (p. 20). In order to gain confidence in his intuitive abilities, the supervisee must feel safe enough to interact with and reveal himself to the supervisor in as open and spontaneous a way as the patient interacts with him. Spotnitz further recommends that students be trained in an experiential way and not within the "framework for purely intellectual learning" (p. 20). Thus interventions will be shaped not only by an intellectual understanding of theory but also by an emotional resonance with the patient informed by intuition.

With this goal in mind, I planned a course that attempted to develop intuitive responsiveness in candidates. Students were instructed to write a synopsis of the week's assigned readings and to connect the content to aspects of their clinical work. The class period was divided into two segments: a discussion of the readings and a discussion of clinical process informed by the readings. As the instructor, I fully accepted whatever was presented and, in this way, modeled a stance of complete openness that did not challenge the validity of their interventions in any way. I, instead, suggested that we investigate together the seemingly inexplicable interventions they reported. In this exercise, my intention was to highlight the idea that everything that happens in a session is a function of the matrix established in the patient/analyst dyad and that communications that arise from nonverbal or intuitive domains inform our interventions.

My interactions with the students were observed and evaluated by two teaching assistants (TAs) who, after class, recorded their reactions to the process and wrote their impressions of the class dynamics. Both TAs were recent graduates of the program and thus were not far removed from their training experience. They had also undergone many years of analysis. Their impressions reflected both strong identifications with the plight of students and clinically mature insights into the difficulties of creating a teaching environment in which intuitive responsiveness could be developed. One TA wrote: "I [think] of how beginning therapists particularly rely on their 'training,' not only the concepts, but also the 'rules,' as they see them, and bypass their own inner sense of how to be with the patient." She also observed that in the case of two male students, one very unsure of his abilities and the other, although more experienced, anxious about his status as a novice analyst, were both

> falling into a kind of rigidity and stiffness because of it. Both men seemed dominated by a sense of rightness and wrongness. The work done with them [in the class] got beyond the superimposed moral code to a deeper exploration of the actual dynamics of the treatment and an evaluation based on the process, rather than the abstract idea of how one should proceed.

She attributed this ability for deeper exploration to the fact that a climate of safety had been created in the classroom and that there was "no right or wrong" answer that needed to be found. Reflecting on Freud's idea about the need to develop a moral code, she wondered: "What is the deepest sense of right or wrong? Is it a cortical function removed from the more primitive instinctual impulses, or is there a way to integrate that sense with intuition that makes it more deeply experienced and felt?"

As an example of how the class had succeeded in helping students learn to trust their intuition, this TA cited a class member who reported feeling shame because her patient was not doing well. Emboldened by the "openness" of the class environment and "because there was no sense that discovery of the 'right' way to proceed was required," the student was then able to reveal that her patient's behavior outside of session had deteriorated—his stealing had become more frequent—and confessed that this behavior surely was proof that she was failing as an analyst. However, in the nonjudgmental, even playful, class atmosphere, observed the TA, this student was for the first time able to give up her habitual defense of "clamming up and withdrawing" and talk openly to the group about her shame and her deeply held beliefs about right and wrong.

It became clear during this course that emotional processing in a safe, nonjudgmental environment facilitated the free expression of student/patient interactions and brought to light elements of intuitive intervention that actually proved helpful to the outcome of the case. In doing the work of analysis, interventions frequently feel, especially to institute candidates, like mistakes. However, when we tell candidates that there is very little to be gained in avoiding an examination of these "mistakes," which may very well be expressions of, as yet, not understood dynamics, we will be on the road to helping them trust their instincts. In case after case, we discovered that a connection could be made between an underlying dynamic in the patient and a feeling reported by the student and that this investigation invariably shed light on the "mistaken" intervention. This new awareness also frequently illuminated countertransference resistances and opened up discussion of transference dynamics.

I recommend that we continue to investigate how best to use our feelings and our intuitive powers in shaping our interventions. The art of psychoanalysis requires that a practitioner's highest cortical center, the repository of theoretical knowledge, be in consonance with the deeper paralimbic center so that our intuitive knowledge may become fully integrated with our theoretical knowledge and thus help us to resonate better with our patients.

REFERENCES

Bollas, C. (1992), *Being a Character: Psychoanalysis and Self Experience.* New York: Harper Collins.

Laquercia, T. (1998), Symbolic imagery: an aspect of unverbalized communication. *Modern Psychoanalysis*, 20:23–33.

Lewis, T., F. Amini & R. Lannon (2001), *A General Theory of Love.* New York: Vintage Books/Random House.

Lomas, P. (1993), *Cultivating Intuition: An Introduction to Psychotherapy.* Northvale, NJ: Jason Aronson.

Meadow, P. W. (1991), Resonating with the pyschotic patient. *Modern Psychoanalysis,* 16:87–103.

——— (2003), *The New Psychoanalysis.* Lanham, MD: Rowman and Littlefield.

Ogden, T. (1982), *Projective Identification and Psychotherapeutic Technique.* New York: Jason Aronson.

Oxford Dictionary (1973), Oxford: Oxford University Press.

Reik, T. (1948), The surprised analyst. *Listening with the Third Ear.* New York: Farrar Strauss. pp. 258–271.

Sheftel, S. (1998), On the patient's need to feel loved. *Modern Psychoanalysis,* 20:35–51.

Spotnitz, H. (1976), Trends in modern psychoanalytic supervision. *Modern Psychoanalysis,* 1:201–217.

——— (2004), *Modern Psychoanalysis of the Schizophrenic Patient.* Second Edition, Enlarged. New York: YBK Publishers.

Spotnitz, H. & P. W. Meadow (1976), *Treatment of the Narcissistic Neuroses.* New York: Manhattan Center for Advanced Psychoanalytic Studies.

Szalita-Pemov, A. B. (1955), The "intuitive process" and its relation to work with schizophrenics. *Journal of the American Psychoanalytic Association,* 3:7–18.

15 West 12th Street
New York, NY 10011
tlaquercia@aol.com

Modern Psychoanalysis
Vol. XXX, No. 1, 2005

Countertransference in Projective Identification and Sadomasochistic States

PAUL GELTNER

Projective identification and sadomasochistic states can create powerful and distinctive types of countertransference in the analytic relationship. In projective identification, the countertransference feeling is the polar opposite of the patient's feeling. In sadosmasochistic states, the counter-transference is characterized by an intense, seemingly inescapable strug-gle in which the analyst experiences the impulse to torture the patient or feels tortured by the patient. The specific types of transferences that induce these types of countertransference are described, along with dis-cussion of how these transference/countertransference configurations operate in the analytic relationship.

Projective identification[1] arises when the patient is unable to tolerate a specific feeling (or fantasy or impulse), expunges it from his emo-tional experience, and induces it in the analyst. Consequently, the patient no longer feels the original feeling but feels its polar opposite instead. Although the patient has ridded himself of the original feeling, he is incapable of letting it go. He remains deeply connected to it through the relationship with the analyst. The analyst, on the other hand, experiences the projected feeling with an engulfing, if not always

---

[1]To be more precise, one should say that the countertransference is the product of projective identification. And to be absolutely precise, one should adopt Grinberg's (1979) terminology and describe the patient's part in the exchange as projective identification and the analyst's part as *introjective identification*, but this terminology has never caught on.

conscious, intensity. Their interpersonal relationship plays out the intrapsychic drama of the patient's inability to accept the intolerable feeling as a part of his self-experience or his emotional identity.

At first sight, the projective identification appears to combine elements of narcissistic and object countertransference. Like a narcissistic induction, the analyst's feeling is originally the patient's feeling. But unlike a narcissistic induction, the analyst and the patient do not share the same feeling in the moment. Like an object induction, the analyst experiences the patient as being different from himself. But unlike an object induction, he feels bonded to the patient through the feeling that has been induced, and he experiences a closeness—usually painful—that is almost inexplicable.

These comparisons only partially illuminate the nature and experience of projective identification. The peculiar combination of separateness and unity—the feeling that the patient and the analyst are each involved with his emotional antithesis—is not midway on a continuum between the narcissistic and object modes of relating but rather is a fundamentally different mode of relatedness. More importantly, it is a mode of relatedness that is essentially defensive. It is possible to relate to other people within the narcissistic or the object matrixes in nondefensive ways.[2] Projective identification, on the other hand, is motivated and shaped exclusively by the need to cope with an intolerable feeling. It usually arises in states of intense overstimulation as an attempt to maintain a degree of intrapsychic equilibrium when more flexible defenses and modes of relating have failed. It is this desperate, last resort quality of projective identification that accounts for its intensity and volatility.

The concept of projective identification was formulated by Klein[3] (1946) as an intrapsychic defense and later developed as a concept that bridged the intrapsychic world with the interpersonal world by Bion (1962), Grotstein (1981), and Ogden (1982). All of these theorists have viewed it as an essential component of both emotional development (normal and pathological) and of the analytic relationship. I agree but with a caveat. Object relations theorists tend to describe all primitive emotional interactions in terms of projective identification and similar

[2]Furthermore, the narcissistic, object, and anaclitic matrices are all compatible with a wide range of defenses; the projective identification matrix is uniquely compatible with the defense of projective identification.

[3]It is worth remembering, but largely irrelevant to this paper, that projective identification can exist purely as an intrapsychic defense without being manifest through emotional induction. The analyst may observe that the patient is in a defensive state of projective identification without necessarily being involved in a transference/countertransference that is shaped by projective identification.

schizoid mechanisms and to describe all induced countertransference as projective identification. In contrast, I view projective identification as a particular form of emotional induction, both as a type of primitive emotional interaction and as a type of countertransference.[4]

Klein (1946) viewed projective identification as a form of splitting, and this can be seen in the lack of complexity in the subjective experience of the countertransference. The feelings are simple and pure, unclouded by subtle emotional shading. What they lack in complexity, they make up for in intensity. The feelings are consuming, flooding, and overwhelming. Projective identification often (but not always) has a life-and-death quality about it that is grossly out of proportion to whatever is being discussed. It is almost impossible for the analyst to avoid being carried away by it, whether or not he is aware of what is happening. Klein viewed projective identification as an infantile attempt to expel unwanted feelings into the mother and a wish to invade her and take control of her from the inside. This often feels literally true; the analyst feels as if he has been invaded and colonized. More than other forms of countertransference, projective identification can feel foreign, like an infection. At the same time, the countertransference feels connected to something deep in the analyst's being, something very real. It is easy to lose control in these states, easy to say and do things that are unanticipated and later regretted.

Projective identification fosters strong feelings of attraction and repulsion within the analytic relationship. Sometimes, the patient and analyst feel magnetically drawn to each other. This attraction is usually painful (at least for one of them), and they never merge in an undifferentiated way as they might in narcissistic countertransference. Other times, however, they draw close in a moment of overwhelming conflict, and then the relationship ends. If, for example, the patient's need to

---

[4]To be more precise: in object relations theory, the concept of projective identification has been used to describe a continuum of phenomena (Hinshelwood, 1992), ranging from states in which projected feeling is shared by the projector and the receiver, flowing fluidly between them, to states in which the feeling is expelled or evacuated into the receiver in a rigid interpersonal configuration. The shared, fluid states are viewed primarily as serving communication functions, while the evacuated states are viewed as serving primarily defensive functions. I am restricting the term to the evacuative/defensive states (most similar to the second and third types described by Rosenfeld (1988, p. 118), and I classify the shared/communicative states as forms of narcissistic countertransference. This is not, I hope, a purely pedantic distinction; rather, I think there are significant differences—experiential, relational, and technical—between a relationship in which the feelings are shared and one in which the feelings are evacuated or expelled, i.e., they are fundamentally different ways of relating to another person. Ogden (1982), the most influential American theorist on the topic, emphasizes both the communicative and the defensive aspects of the process. I would classify some of his examples as narcissistic countertransference and others as projective identification.

expel the feeling is particularly strong, he will project the feeling into the analyst, then reject him and leave the treatment. Similarly, if the analyst cannot tolerate the projected feeling due to his subjective limitations, he may reject the patient, either overtly or covertly.

The relationship between the analyst's feeling and the patient's is invariant: they are polar opposites. If the analyst feels powerless, the patient feels powerful. If the analyst feels agitated, the patient feels calm. If the analyst feels aggression, the patient feels like a victim. If the analyst feels like he needs the patient, the patient feels that he is a parasite. If the analyst feels wise and competent, the patient feels stupid and helpless.

This polar opposition between the patient's feelings and the analyst's feelings is an important hallmark of projective identification and distinct from the disjunctions that occur in either narcissistic or object countertransference. While the analyst does not experience the same overt feeling as the patient in an incongruent narcissistic countertransference, the analyst's feeling is rarely the opposite of the patient's feeling, either in content or intensity. On the other hand, polar opposition between the analyst's feelings and the patient's can occur in object countertransference. In object countertransference, however, the focus of the analyst's feelings is the patient, but in projective identification, the analyst's feelings are about himself and the patient in equal measure. If the analyst is drawn to the patient, he may feel as if the patient fills a void and makes him feel whole in a way that he has never felt before. If he hates the patient, he may feel as if the patient is everything he hates in another person, the living antithesis of his values or choices.

Because the essence of projective identification is to have a feeling opposite to that of the patient, it is not clear whether it can ever be incongruent in the way other forms of countertransference are. The difference between, and the relationship between, the analyst and patient's feeling are always visible. It can, however, be extremely subtle, requiring close observation.

Projective identifications can occur in different patterns within the analysis. Most of my experience and that of most of my colleagues and supervisees have been with projective identification that arises in fairly discrete episodes within a relationship dominated by other transference/countertransference configurations. Sometimes, projective identification arises regularly around circumscribed feeling clusters. In certain borderline and narcissistic patients, it is the dominant mode of relating in the analysis and the dominant form of countertransference. Similarly, there is a variant form of projective identification—the sadomasochistic induction—that usually becomes an all-enveloping mode of relating.

Some Typical Examples

This example of projective identification occurred in the first session with a patient who had been referred to me early in my career specifically because I was accepting low-fee referrals. She was tall and beautiful, even dazzling. Her clothes were stunning, her voice lovely, her manner casual and self-assured—not exactly what I had been expecting of a low-fee referral. She told me quickly that she was an interior designer. She specialized in country French interiors because she had excellent furniture contacts in Provence. She was an alcoholic, in recovery, and very committed to working the Twelve Steps. When I asked what she hoped to get from therapy, she said her sponsor had recommended it. She thought it would be a good idea because "everyone can stand a little improvement." She had recently broken up with a long-term boyfriend, and although she was over it (the break-up had been all for the best), she felt she still thought about him too much. Apart from that, there was precious little discussion of any problems she might have. She spent most of the session telling me about her good friends, most of whom were famous, and those that weren't she discussed as if they were well-kept secrets, known only to the cognoscenti. She looked a bit askance at my office and made an ever so slightly dismissive remark about the art on the walls. At one point I asked how the session had been for her. She looked at me directly for the first time since she walked in and told me that I seemed "pleasant enough and the fee is certainly reasonable, not that you don't deserve more when I can afford it, which I expect will be *very* soon."

In retrospect (and no doubt to the reader), the patient's condescension, grandiosity, and arrogance scream out. But the experience of being in the room with her, under the active influence of the induction, was very different. I was intimidated from the first shake of her exquisite head, the first glimpse of her silk blouse. I immediately felt shabby, unsophisticated, and cheap. My work as an analyst felt pedestrian and completely unglamorous in comparison to decorating fantastic apartments and country homes. And she knew all of those famous people that I had only read about. Her problems seemed minor, yet exalted —the romance of being a high-powered alcoholic in recovery. The fact that she was completely broke seemed to be a meaningless blip on a rising graph.

In contrast, my own problems with depression and self-assertiveness, of which I was painfully aware, were utterly banal. Her clothes were better than mine, her friends were better than mine, and her taste was better than mine. Even though her French was worse than mine, which was obvious from the few phrases she tossed off, there was still something classier about it, something more exotic about the fact that she *didn't* speak as fluently as I did. I was a working stiff, a boring professional with a tacky office with schlock art on the walls, the kind people sought out if they had a problem like bleeding gums or plantar warts but didn't have much money. I assumed that once she got herself on her feet financially she would drop me immediately and move on to an older, probably famous, Upper East Side analyst with a gray beard, an exquisite silk rug, and a complete set of Freud in German. I was filled with envy, competitiveness, and wretched feelings of inferiority. In every respect I was the dark side of her gloriously silver moon. Need I add that I was completely miserable by the time the session ended?

This intensity of feeling lasted about four sessions, and then it began to change. I became more comfortable. Although she did not abandon her overtly narcissistic posture, her tone changed considerably, and she began a long, slow process of verbalizing layers of self-hatred, most of which were centered, almost word for word, on exactly the same types of feelings that I had experienced in that first session. Gradually she took back the feelings that had been projected into me and integrated them into her character.

This example shows all of the essential characteristics of projective identification. First, the polar opposition of her feelings and mine. Second, the intensity of the countertransference. In this case, the countertransference was clearly congruent with her demeanor, but I must confess that this was not obvious at the time. In fact, I would have said that she was perfectly charming; it wasn't her fault if I was an insecure little schlepper.

The fact that this occurred in a first session is also something I have found to be typical of projective identification. Indeed, I have seen more examples of projective identifications in the first session or first few sessions than in any other part of the treatment. Many patients who do not relate primarily in this mode will do so in the first few sessions. I suspect that the stress of meeting the analyst and beginning the process of describing one's feelings leaves the patient vulnerable and stimulates a defensive regression.

And sometimes the feelings generated in this process are so strong it aborts the analysis altogether. This can be seen in another example, again the first session with a low-fee patient. He was very serious and explained at the beginning of the session that before he got into discussing his problems, he wanted to discuss my qualifications. Although this is, in itself, not an unusual or unreasonable request, I felt myself freezing up almost immediately. He proceeded to "outline" what he wanted from me. First, of course, my degrees, including the names of the schools, the programs, the specific classes I had taken, grades, preferably going back to my undergraduate years. Then, he would need recommendations from teachers and supervisors as well as current and former patients. Finally, he would want to discuss some of my relevant life experiences (he didn't elaborate on what these might be) and would need to know my favorite novels, philosophers, clinical theoreticians, and political thinkers. After all, he would need to know a little bit about me if he was going to tell me about himself.

All of this proceeded slowly over the course of the session, during which I became increasingly filled with panic. The demands felt absolutely overwhelming, and there was a dread certainty that I was going to fail—and then what?! I made some feeble attempts to explore his requests, but I was crumbling, and I'm sure he knew it. His tone was deadly serious, perfectly calm throughout. The more anxious I got, the more controlled he became. Finally, he looked at me and said, "It seems obvious that I am going to need a very special person to work with me and that you are not it." (He was right, of course, but not for the reasons that he consciously thought.) He got up and decisively left the office. I felt as though I had been crushed and left for trash.

This was the only contact I had with the patient, so I cannot be sure that it was, in fact, projective identification. I knew from the person who had referred him that he was unemployed, depressed, and friendless. Yet even more than in the first example, there had been no discussion of his problems or of what he wanted from the treatment—certainly an unexpected outcome of an initial analytic session. Once I could start to think clearly again, my hypothesis was that he had ridded himself of all of his feelings of worthlessness, incompetence, and anxiety by inducing them in me, allowing him to feel competent and in control. Our interchange bore all the telltale signs. Again, there was the sharp dichotomy between my feeling and the patient's: he was calm, hypercontrolled; I was consumed with anxiety.

Another example occurred about a year and a half into the treatment of an extremely volatile, paranoid woman. She had a long history of starting fights and then being physically hurt. In the first session, she had strongly objected to my writing down her name and address. In the event that she ever had to punch me, she didn't want there to be any paperwork proving she had ever been in the office. The early months of treatment were characterized by mutual distrust.

After a few months, however, we fell into a more comfortable rhythm as she settled into talking to me about her life and her problems. I was quite comfortable listening to her without any striking countertransference reactions. At times she would flair up and become extremely challenging, insisting that I couldn't possibly understand her because I was a younger sibling and she was an older one, and there was no common ground between us. But even in the face of these conflicts, the emotional climate in the analysis was rather lukewarm for both of us, which was a productive state of affairs. The dynamic began to shift again as she talked increasingly about how she felt exploited by everyone. It was all give and no take. Nobody ever gave her anything, including me. She frequently criticized me for being a cheap Jew.[5] I felt unsympathetic to her feelings of being exploited. It wasn't clear to me who was exploiting her or what they were getting out of it. I suspected that I was having feelings similar to her mother's, whom she described as being chronically unsympathetic.

One day she began the session by telling me that it was high time we did something about the fee. The situation had been going on long enough, and it had to change. At first, I thought she had finally realized it was too low and she was going to raise it. I greedily began to wonder whether it would be doubled to two dollars or even go up to five. Her agenda, however, was otherwise. She had concluded that the fee was too high. It was time for it to be lowered to zero dollars because I was in a training program. She was getting the benefit of the treatment, and I was getting the benefit of the experience and the credit; for me to get paid on top of that was excessive and obviously exploitative. Atypically for her, she wasn't shouting or swearing; her reasoning was clear and lucid, her affect strong yet calm. I felt as if my life-force, all of my vital energy, had been tapped with a needle and was being drained off into her. All the while, I was fully aware of her mildly malevolent smile. She was a serene yet determined bloodsucker, and I was fading into oblivion.

It is clear in this case that she induced the feeling that she had been talking about prior to this session—the feeling of being exploited although exploitation was hardly the word for it. She had attempted to cope with it by talking about it, but when that had not worked (proba-

---

[5] Her fee was one dollar; I frequently had the urge to tell her that she was right—Jews didn't come any cheaper than that.

bly my emotional response to her had not be adequate to her needs), she responded with this projective identification.

A therapist described a projective identification that took place with a girl who was treated at a school for conduct-disordered teenagers. The girl's home was seriously chaotic; she called it a zoo and referred to her mother and siblings as animals. She was always in some sort of trouble at school and seemed to have some degree of concern about whether she would be able to control herself. The therapist was somewhat concerned about her, but not more than for the other kids, all of whom were in similar situations. One day the girl arrived in a gleeful, exuberant, silly state. She and her sister had just pulled off an unusually serious prank: they had set off the fire sprinklers in the cafeteria. The patient was smiling about it and said she knew she was going to get caught. The therapist became overwhelmed with anxiety. "What's going to happen to you?" she asked. The patient told her not to worry. She was already in a "jail-school." What else could they do to her? In her more rational mind, the therapist was thinking that something really should be done with this girl because she was completely out of control. But most of her feelings were focused on, "Oh my god, she's going to get in trouble. What am *I* going to do?" She kept trying to get the patient to recognize the seriousness of the situation, and the patient kept laughing and telling her there was nothing to worry about. The patient was filled with manic (in the Kleinian, not the psychiatric, sense of the term) triumph while all of the patient's anxiety was projected into the therapist,

The following is an example of a projective identification that was less volatile and recurred regularly during a long treatment. The patient was a young man who was preoccupied with dichotomies in all areas of his self-image. He was quite attractive, stylishly dressed and groomed, but he usually looked hunched over and collapsed, like a decrepit child. Referred by a friend of his who had heard me speak at a conference, he idealized me from the moment he set eyes on me. He saw me as powerful, wise, and compassionate. He wanted me as a role model. He just knew that I lived the kind of life that he didn't. But he didn't think I could really be a role model because he was so hopelessly weak, stupid, and selfish he could never be the way I was. His words were like a magic spell on me. As he lay on the couch, I had the feeling he was frail and helpless, the limp husk of a man who was ineffective, incompetent, and lost. I, on the other hand, felt like a uniquely radiant being, a healing god, a psychoanalytic Apollo. The mere touch of my spirit on this poor waif and he would spring to life like a desert flower after the rain. In spite of his talk about how wonderful I was, he also had fantasies that I could barely tolerate his presence, that I sprayed the couch with deodorant after he left the sessions. While I never had exactly those feelings about him, I often thought (with a touch of sadism) that his lovers (he infrequently had casual lovers) would think he was completely insane once they got to know him.

In this case, the patient had projected all the good feelings onto me and retained all the bad feelings in and about himself. As time went on, he increasingly attributed aggressive, persecutory feelings to me and felt that he was a victim.

Another example of projective identification was described by a supervisee in the case of a male patient who displayed many of the features of the narcissistic personality as described by Kernberg (1975): he was haughty, contemptuous, lacking in empathy, and had a pronounced inability to tolerate dependency feelings. However, as therapy went on, he was increasingly able to discuss feelings of vulnerability and even to understand, on a deeply emotional level, how he resorted to aggression against others when he felt unsafe. After about three years, he revealed that he had been seeing a doctor for about six months about prostate problems. He was rather matter of fact about the whole thing, and during those matter-of-fact moments the therapist was equally blasé about the matter. His tone changed, however, after he got the biopsy results back. He laughed cynically and described how the doctor had told him, in an incompetent way, that he had never seen a biopsy like that. There were a number of unusual cells in it, but he didn't know why or what they meant, and he would have to go in for a more invasive test. The therapist was overwhelmed with panic and had the impression that the patient's laughter intensified as her anxiety rose. The patient began to speak derisively about a friend he considered to be a weakling. He added, also laughingly, that he had told his parents about it and that they had been terrified.

Here, the patient projected all the fear and the panic about his medical condition into those around him and retained in himself a feeling of denial and manic triumph over weakness and fear. On the surface, this case appears similar to a narcissistic induction described earlier. In both cases, the analyst is concerned about the patient's health, and the patient appears to be unconcerned. In both cases, a defense is operating, but the nature of the defense is different because it is grounded in, or expressed through, a completely different type of object relation.[6]

In the case of the narcissistic countertransference, the ego boundaries between the patient and the analyst are open and fluid, with feel-

[6]Does the defense shape the type of object relation? Or does the type of object relation shape the defense? I doubt that this question is solvable. However, it again illustrates the intrinsically defensive nature of the projective identification object relationship.

ings flowing in each direction such that the analyst readily experiences the patient's anxiety. The patient is defended against the anxiety, and has intellectualized it in a way that has made his conscious experience of it muted or neutralized but not disowned. Nor does the patient feel contempt for those who feel anxiety. He does not distance himself from the analyst as the analyst experiences the feeling. Rather, he relates to the analyst as a part of himself and uses emotional induction within the relationship to communicate a feeling that he cannot consciously experience. As the analyst experiences the feeling, the patient is usually able to reintegrate the feeling into his own experience.[7]

In projective identification, on the other hand, the patient has actively disowned the anxiety, expelled it into the analyst, and experiences it not as a part of himself, but a part of the analyst. This does, of course, communicate the feeling to the analyst; but more importantly, the patient needs the analyst to feel it so that he doesn't have to feel it. Indeed, once the analyst has the feeling, the patient defends further against it by despising the analyst's weakness. The patient uses the interpersonal relationship to maintain his psychic equilibrium.

Sadomasochistic Inductions

Sadomasochistic dynamics are induced by a transference/countertransference matrix in which the key element is the compulsion to hurt and be hurt. Actually, the idea of hurting and being hurt is too weak: torture and torment more accurately convey the relentlessly excruciating psychic pain involved in sadomasochistic inductions. The analyst may feel either like the tormentor or the tormented; most often he feels like both—either simultaneously or in alternation. Most commonly, the analyst does not initially experience sadistic impulses towards the patient and feels tormented when it becomes clear that the patient feels tortured by him despite his benevolent conscious intentions. Over time, he may experience unforeseen sadistic gratification when he sees that he has hurt the patient, or he may even have fully sadistic conscious impulses, usually in the form of revenge fantasies. Of course, the analyst may also experience fully conscious sadistic impulses early on in the dynamic, but I have found this to be rare except in work with extremely masochistic patients.

[7]As mentioned in footnote 4, an object relations theorist would call this healthy projective identification.

I'm not exactly sure what mode of relatedness underlies sado-masochistic inductions. Sadomasochistic themes can be expressed in the object matrix, and the subjective experience of the countertransference can also be similar to the intensely negative symmetrical narcissistic configurations (Geltner, 2002). However, there is an intensity to the more purely sadomasochistic dynamics that is more similar to projective identification as well as a degree of unrelenting struggle, which seems to make it impossible for either the patient or the analyst to let go, that feels qualitatively different from either the narcissistic or object states.

Being immersed in a sadomasochistic countertransference is exactly like being part of an endlessly quarreling couple, and the dynamic is identical. Frequently, the impulses to hurt or be hurt occur in an almost pure form, rooted in the patient's life history but unconnected to other dynamic issues. But they can also be melded to a number of develop-mental conflicts, either separately or in combination.

One such conflict is the struggle for emotional resources. Who will get his needs met and how? Will one person's needs destroy the other's? This struggle is played out against the assumption that it is not possible for both parties to get their needs met.

Another is the struggle over merger and separateness. How can one be close without being engulfed? How can one be close without being abandoned? Engulfment means the obliteration of the self. Abandonment means death or intolerable levels of anxiety. Again, the struggle is based on the unstated emotional assumption that no middle ground is possible.

Then, there is the struggle for control. Who will control whom? How will this be accomplished or resisted? What does this mean in the relationship?

These are normal developmental struggles that are not primarily about hurting or being hurt and are not usually experienced in a sado-masochistic context. When they become fused with sadomasochism, however, the intensity of the dynamic increases dramatically, and the sadomasochistic dimensions of the dynamic take on an overriding importance. I suspect there are a number of possible reasons this might occur. The parent(s), with whom these struggles were originally enact-ed, may have been overtly sadomasochistic and infused the struggles with sadomasochism right from the start. Or, the parent or the child may have been extremely sensitive to these struggles, resulting in a degree of pain and torment that eventually overshadowed the original issues in the child's attempts to come to terms with it.[8]

---

[8] It is often unclear whether the sadomasochism is serving as a defense against these other issues or whether these other issues are serving as a defense against the sadomasochism.

However, the reasons for all of this are by no means clear. While the essence of the repetition compulsion is to repeat all early experiences, good or bad, most repetitions—even extremely negative ones—do not evolve into the distinctive frenzy of torture that is characteristic of sadomasochism. At the same time, sadomasochism is an extremely compelling dynamic. Many people who do not ordinarily engage in sadomasochistic repetitions can be easily induced into such a relationship by somebody who is strongly sadomasochistic.

Another important dynamic that is commonly associated with sadomasochism is, of course, sexuality. Many would argue that sadomasochism is an intrinsically sexual, or sexualized, mode of relating. I have often experienced sadomasochistic inductions with patients who were or had been involved in overt sexually sadomasochistic relationships or behavior. Furthermore, I have also seen cases in which patients who were prone to sadomasochistic transferences that were not overtly sexual—both in their outside lives and in the analytic relationship—experienced a vastly diminished need for these kinds of relationships after allowing themselves to feel overtly sexual sadomasochistic fantasies or, in some cases, after deciding to engage in such activities. These cases certainly suggest that sexual feelings can underlie seemingly non-sexual sadomasochism.

However, not every patient who engages in sadomasochistic behavior induces sadomasochistic countertransference. More importantly, I have seen many cases in which there wasn't even a hint of sexuality in the sadomasochism. There are wells of sadomasochism in the human character unrelated to sexuality.

Although sadomasochistic inductions can arise sporadically, once they occur, they frequently dominate the treatment for a period of time. They also have a distinctive quality of completely enveloping the interaction between the patient and the analyst. While other transference/countertransference matrices can be extremely powerful, it is usually possible—at least for a moment—for the patient and the analyst to step out of the matrix and experience each other in ways that are not totally colored by the it.[9] In sadomasochistic inductions, on the other hand, it is almost impossible for either party to escape from the cycle of torture. Everything either one of them says takes on a sadomasochistic meaning, no matter its conscious intention. It is impossible to step out of the rain. An example occurred with the patient I mentioned earlier, who

[9]This is not to say that it is necessarily beneficial for them to step out of the transference/countertransference matrix, e.g., for the analyst to address the unafflicted parts of the patient's ego with the (presumably) unafflicted parts of his ego; it may be therapeutic or it may not be, depending on the case. The important point here is experiential, not technical.

wanted to lower my fee. She frequently came quite early for the appointment, and she found it demeaning that she had to wait for the session time. Although I usually had a patient before her, I had always started her sessions on time because at that point in my career I viewed such regularity as crucial to the analytic frame. I persisted with this even though it meant that I could have been a little less rushed if I did start early.

One day, however, I was free the session before I was to see her. I impulsively decided that it was rigid and doctrinaire to make her wait when it wasn't necessary.[10] Besides, I thought it might be nice to have a few extra minutes to get to my next destination.

Flush with the feeling of liberating myself from superfluous constraints, I asked if she wanted to start early.

She glared at me. "Start early?" she asked, "And when would we stop?"

"After 50 minutes—as usual," I replied, instantly regretting my suggestion.

"So we wouldn't run any longer?"

"No," I said.

"So you want to get rid of me—and you would get to go home early. Absolutely not. I want to start at the usual time!"

Was I trying to get rid of her early? In some ways, yes. I did want to leave earlier if I could. On the other hand, I also thought that she would want to start early, in light of her previous complaints. Yet she experienced it as if I was depriving her of an opportunity to start early and spend more time together as if I were gratuitously rejecting her. It was one more way in which I was in control of her, humiliating her, dictating the terms of our relationship to her. In response to her, I also felt humiliated and controlled—as if I had suddenly been unmasked and as if she had suddenly gotten the upper hand, and I was not in her power. And I felt furiously misunderstood. We both felt tortured in this exchange—and the feeling persisted through the rest of the session in a similar vein. We each felt tortured, accused, or attacked by the other, no matter what either one of us said.

A longer running example of a sadomasochistic countertransference occurred with a patient who had become very dissatisfied with our work and also with his appointment time. It's hard to know which came first. He needed an evening appointment, and I only had one particular time available for a long time. He speculated about why this was the case. He had two theories: either I was a beginner—i.e., a weakling—

---

[10] I eventually reached the same conclusion, but less impulsively and in more appropriate clinical circumstances.

and couldn't get another hour because I couldn't get anything that I needed in life; or I had lots of time available, but I wouldn't give it to him because I wanted to teach him a lesson. As his resentment grew, he denigrated the treatment in general, insisting that I was no use to him or to anyone. My frustration grew in lockstep with his. The fact was that I was locked into a very tight schedule, and there were elements in the situation that made me think that he was right in thinking that I was a weakling who couldn't get what he needed. (But that was not the whole story, and I knew it.) And on the other hand, his idea that I would not give him the time because I was withholding was not initially true, but as time went on I felt less and less interested in accommodating him. At times he would complain about everything I had ever done or not done. I was completely useless. I was incompetent. He was getting his life together, and he certainly didn't need the likes of me holding him back. "You know," he said, "I can't think of a single thing that you ever did or said that helped me even a little bit. I don't think you have enough training or experience to help anyone. How old are you, anyway? Have you even lived long enough to understand someone else's problems?" These moments were blistering, and I felt as if every word were true.

Then at other times he valued the treatment and felt close to me. But these moments usually ended with his moaning, "If only I didn't have to come on Tuesday. You know that Tuesday is the only day of the week that is terrible for me. Anything but Tuesday would be fine. Why, oh why, can't you give me a different time?" (Over time, this was actually untrue; I had offered other times, and he had refused them as being even worse.) Because I actually couldn't give him the time he wanted, I felt free of guilt in enjoying his frustration. It was payback for all the nasty things he said about me. I even had fantasies of saying to him. "I don't have another time. I'll never have another time. You will be stuck with this time for the rest of your life!" The sadism came into further bloom when I later had a couple of dreams about him, which I interpreted as his inviting me to rape him and my feeling the impulse to oblige him.

His complaining reached the point where he was ready to leave treatment, to which I responded with what amounted to an order to stay in treatment until we had talked this out. Soon after this interchange I was able to give him a time that he wanted, and the biographical material that underlay this dynamic emerged. The first elements were memories of cold brutality that were woven into his daily care by his parents. His mother would twist his arm too hard as she dressed him or casually knock his face with her elbow. The next element was a relationship that he had with one of his university teachers when he was a freshman. She had initiated the relationship, which rapidly became sadomasochistic. He described having rough sex with her and constantly threatening to leave her while she begged him to stay with her. Several years later, he began to remember being sexually abused at around five years old by a babysitter that had cared for him while his family was living in Thailand. He had loved this woman, but she had also been very strict with him, and the sexual abuse was sadomasochistic. When he was a little older, after she had left, he had gone through a period of being sadistic to animals. He had originally come to me because he had a pattern of being fired from his jobs. All of these themes were repeated in the transference and the countertransference.

Sadomasochistic inductions can revolve more narrowly around the quantity and quality of the analyst's emotional availability to the patient, both in and out of the session. When the manifest issue is about the analyst's availability in the session, it usually takes the form of the patient wanting more from the analyst—more interpretations, more talking, more self-disclosure, more sympathy, more understanding— more, more, more. When the analyst tries to satisfy the patient, the patient complains that he has done it (whatever it is) wrong. Or he hasn't done it enough. Or it is too little, too late. Or he didn't really do it at all.

Should the analyst actually do exactly what the patient wants, the patient often ends up frustrated and hurt in a different way. A colleague described a patient who was preoccupied with exercise, who said that she needed to know what kind of exercise the analyst did. She insisted that exercise was paradigmatic of how someone took care of herself. Since she was dedicated to taking excellent care of herself, she needed to know that the analyst was taking care of herself as well. The patient's demands were relentless, and the analyst initially met them with equally relentless exploration. The patient felt tortured by the analyst's refusal to give her the answer, and the analyst felt tortured by the patient's refusal to be satisfied with analytic abstinence.

As the weeks went on, the patient convinced the analyst that she wouldn't be able to stay in treatment unless the analyst disclosed this information. The analyst felt that she had to either give her the information or lose the case.

At the same time, she decided that she may have been withholding with the patient; after all, she was as dedicated to her own exercise regimen as the patient was to hers. Perhaps the patient's need to know was based on a narcissistic need to know that the analyst was like her. So, the next time the patient asked her about it, she described what she did at the gym: two days of boxing and three days of free weights.

The patient was horrified. She did tai chi and yoga. How could the analyst engage in activities that were so destructive to her body, so disruptive to her hormonal system, and so inimical to any sort of spiritual development? The patient said she felt physically ill at the thought of the analyst lying on a weight bench and pumping iron. How could she possibly be in analysis with someone like that? She felt completely betrayed.

The analyst was equally horrified. Her decision hadn't been impulsive. She had carefully thought about it for weeks, and yet it appeared that she had injured the patient with this communication. She also felt somewhat gratified (guiltily) by the patient's reaction, as if to say: "See, you wanted it, you got it. Now how does it feel?" And she also felt personally stung by the patient's describing her own cherished activities as some sort of Nazi self-mutilation ritual. Unfortunately, the case continued to deteriorate, with the patient feeling increasingly tortured by the analyst and the analyst feeling completely overwhelmed by the intensity of the patient's response,[11] and ended in termination.

Also common are sadomasochistic struggles over the analyst's availability outside the sessions. The patient feels that he needs, wants, or depends on the analyst's presence and wants to be able to reach him off-hours, on holidays, or over vacations. And so the struggle begins. The patient feels that the analyst is cruelly withholding. He acts and feels as though he is weak, helpless, and at the analyst's mercy. He feels tortured when he cannot get in contact with the analyst whenever he wants; in session (or in interminable phone messages) he tortures the analyst with stories of how tortured he was. Or the patient is filled with righteous indignation. He complains mercilessly about the cruelty, the sheer injustice of the analytic set-up; the analyst has all the power, and the patient just has to take it!

The analyst, in turn, feels victimized by the patient's complaints. Or he may feel a sadistic gratification in the patient's frustration that is often masked by self-righteous thoughts like: the patient has to learn to accept limits; he must learn to put his feelings into words even when he is not gratified; this will help him to experience his feelings of deprivation consciously, instead of acting them out (translation—this will teach him a good lesson!). He might also defend against feeling the sadomasochistic arousal with thoughts like: I'm better at setting limits than I used to be, I don't let myself get walked over any more; if he

[11]This case is given as an example of a sadomasochistic transference/countertransference and is not offered as evidence for or against the value of self-disclosure in general. While this disclosure was not, obviously, an example of good technique—it seems probable that the case would have taken the same direction if analyst had not disclosed the information.

doesn't like it, he can always go to another analyst, that's the bottom line on who I am and what I can do.

Attempts to gratify the patient seldom work because the patient's demands escalate. Setting limits firmly right from the start usually doesn't work either because the problem is only partially about limits. Nor is it only about how much contact the patient actually needs, or about helping the patient to put his feelings into words. These are the types of cases in which the patient's[12] issues about dependency and emotional availability were initially experienced in the context of a sadomasochistic relationship, and the problem remains until the sadomasochistic component is worked through.

REFERENCES

Bion, W.R. (1962), *Learning from Experience*. London: Karnac Books.

Geltner, P. (2002), Varieties of object countertransference. *Annals of Modern Psychoanalysis*, 1:215–250.

—— (2003), The dynamics of narcissistic countertransference. *Annals of Modern Psychoanalysis*, 2:187–213.

Grinberg, L. (1979), Countertransference and projective counteridentification. *Contemporary Psychoanalysis*, 15: 226–247.

Grotstein, J. (1981), *Splitting and Projective Identification*. Northvale, NJ: Jason Aronson.

Hinshelwood, R.D. (1992), *Clinical Klein*. London: Free Association Books.

Kernberg, O. (1975), *Borderline Conditions and Pathological Narcissism*. Northvale, NJ: Jason Aronson.

Klein, M. (1946), Notes on some schizoid mechanisms. *Envy and Gratitude and Other Works: 1946-1963*. London: Karnac Books, 1993.

Ogden. T.H. (1982), *Projective Identification and Psychotherapeutic Technique*. Northvale, NJ: Jason Aronson.

Rosenfeld, H. (1988), Contribution to the psychopathology of psychotic states: the importance of projective identification in the ego structure and the object relations of the psychotic patient. *Melanie*

---

[12]I should add here that this dynamic is also fairly frequently induced by the analyst and is an expression of the analyst's need to repeat a sadomaschistic relationship around his emotional availability. With the exception of patients who are clearly borderline, I have not seen this type of outrageously intense struggle occur very often.

Klein Today: Developments in Theory and Practice. Volume I. E. Bott-Spillius, ed. London: Routledge.

24 E. 12th St. #505
New York, NY 10003
pgeltner@earthlink.net

Modern Psychoanalysis
Vol. XXX, No. 1, 2005

Jekyll and Hyde: A Literary Forerunner to Freud's Discovery of the Unconscious

BARBARA D'AMATO

Nineteenth-century writers such as Robert Louis Stevenson in "The Strange Case of Dr. Jekyll and Mr. Hyde" struggled with dream material and duality in man. Freud, conceptualizing psychoanalysis in this milieu, was enormously influenced by literary writers, who he believed were in tune with the unconscious. Through Freud's Interpretation of Dreams *and Stevenson's novella, the link between an author's unconscious and his written work is explored.*

If nature had intended that sleepers should do what they dreamed, persons on going to bed would always have to be tied, otherwise they would commit more follies in their dreams than any madman ever did.

Cicero (106–43 B.C.)

"The Strange Case of Dr. Jekyll and Mr. Hyde" (Stevenson, 1978), along with a multitude of nineteenth-century gothic and detective stories and autobiographies, made a significant contribution to the intellectual climate in which Freud (1900) would write *The Interpretation of Dreams* (Thomas, 1990). Various English writers— the Brontës, Charles Dickens, Thomas DeQuincey, Arthur Conan Doyle, as well as Stevenson—were working through to a literary and cultural understanding of intrapsychic processes that Freud would extrapolate from, develop, refine, and eventually define as the unconscious. Such authors were making use of the dream in fiction as a vehi-

© 2005 CMPS/*Modern Psychoanalysis*, Vol. 30, No. 1

cle for reckoning with unconscious conflicts; indeed, from the dawn of civilization writers and philosophers have used dream material as a portal to exploring human motivation and the possible existence of an internal life (Wolf, 1952; van de Castle, 1994), Plato (1955), Aristotle (1936, 1941), Lucretius (1968), Cicero (2001), Thomas Aquinas (1225–1275), Descartes (1596–1650), and Voltaire (1694–1778) can be cited among many of Freud's forerunners in the investigation of mankind's evidently conflicting inner desires. Sharpe (1937), Jung (1968), Bion (1962), Ogden (2001), Quinodoz (2002), Segal (1991), Woods & Greenhouse (1974), Spotnitz & Meadow (1976), Meadow (1984), Hobson (1988, 1999, 2003), Hobson and McCarley (1977), Hobson and Leonard (2001), Solms, (1995, 1997, 1999) and Winson (1985, 1990) are among those who have followed him.

In the latter half of the nineteenth century, the psychic and intellectual climate in Freud's Vienna was becoming ripe for the conception and delivery of psychoanalysis. A foundation that allowed for the discovery of an intrapsychic life had been laid one brick at a time over many centuries by thinkers and writers who preceded Freud. Robert Louis Stevenson (1978) was one such architect, (unconsciously) using dream material to portray the existence of a human unconscious in "The Strange Case of Dr Jekyll and Mr Hyde."

"Jekyll and Hyde" embraces the notion of duality in man and the presence of unconscious impulses. Inspired by an extraordinary dream, Stevenson's fictional story reveals his psychic conflicts as well as his curiosity concerning the duality of man as a universal experience. So, too, does Freud (1900) reveal his innermost psychic conflicts along with a systematic study of man's duality in his "novel," *The Interpretation of Dreams.* An analysis of Freud's personal conflicts, based on dreams associated with the writing and publication of *The Interpretation of Dreams,* and an analysis of "Jekyll and Hyde," based on Stevenson's dream, will demonstrate similarities in the psyches of both writers.

By the mid-1850s, the political and historical setting in England was one of instability. As many of the British began to question the role of England's world domination and its failing programs of colonization, England could be described as a nation suffering from a deep-seated internal conflict (Thomas, 1990). Was England to rule the world, or did individual nations have a right to their own destinies? In a parallel psychic conflict, was the individual ruled by external forces or an inner self-determination? Were dreams the result of supernatural events coming down upon the dreamer, or were dreams the products of men's minds? If dreams came from the minds of men, what was driving them?

These existential questions permeated the collective literary uncon-scious of Freud's time.

Two fundamental premises structure this paper. One is that authors fictionalize their own conflicts in an unconscious effort of working through, and Freud is no exception. Secondly, the climate in Europe in the late 1880s was readying itself for Freud's discovery of the uncon-scious. Stevenson, in "Jekyll and Hyde," was struggling with the con-cept of duality in man. Stevenson queried whether opposing forces coexist in the individual. The manifestations of good and evil had his-torically been clearly separated through religious doctrine and autocrat-ic rule. Individuals were polarized into one category or another. As Freud would eventually discover, we are each the sum total of our instincts. Along with love and life forces, hatred and destructive impulses exist simultaneously. Some individuals successfully fuse these drives while others repress or defend against particular unwanted aspects of their internal experiences. "Jekyll and Hyde" demonstrates one author's interpretation of what can happen when the expression of one force is fully denied. A pathological split occurs. An analysis of Stevenson's novella demonstrates his unconscious understanding of the true nature of man and the instinctual forces that lie within. He most likely did not understand that his own destructive drives were leading him towards death. Meanwhile, Freud would provide a systematic the-ory that would eventually culminate in an understanding of the destruc-tivity, which would be of little value to him in avoiding his own slow death from cancer.

The Mother in Freud's Life and Writing

Amalia Freud adored her first-born son Sigmund. In return he con-sciously idealized her (Jones, 1961; Gay, 1988; Margolis, 1996). Yet his theory does not even vaguely suggest that he was the product of any preoedipal maternal ministrations or preverbal conflict or that he ever harbored negative feelings for his mother. In Freud's personal life and in his libido theory, the mother as an object becomes significant only at the oedipal level. She is revealed as an object of sexual desire, a figure in primal scene memory and fantasy (Freud, 1918), producing rivalry between the son and his father in the family romance (Freud, 1909). Stevenson's novella is also devoid of mothers and virtually ignores the female gender. Both Stevenson's fictional story and Freud's theory share a mutual need and/or preference for men.

Freud is cathected to fathers, and his writings cite numerous male transference figures. In a description of one such narcissistic transference, Gay (1988) reports Freud's referring to Fliess as "the only Other, the alter" (p. 56). Freud's intense transference relationships were reserved for males. Shakespeare, Rabelais, Swift, Zola, Schiller, Goethe, and Tennyson, an exclusive array of male writers, hold positions of great significance for Freud. He quoted the works of these men as he revealed their influence upon him. Writers, however, dwell in a world of words. Words symbolically represent food, the breast, and the early mother. Freud was unconsciously connected to, or longing for, the early mother (through love or hate) whom he would inexorably exclude from his theories.

Freud's "Novel": The Interpretation of Dreams

Freud (1900) reveals much of his own psyche in his early psychoanalytic publication, *The Interpretation of Dreams*, analyzing 46 of his own dreams in which he reveals himself in a first-person narrative (Thomas, 1990). Aware of the self-revealing nature of dreams, Freud offers a disclaimer when he reaches a certain analytical depth in the Botanical Monograph (p. 169). This dream, among other conflicts, suggests Freud's internal struggle with self-worth as it relates to his success in publishing: "For reasons with which we are not concerned, I shall not pursue the interpretation of this dream any further, but will merely indicate the direction in which it lay" (p.173). Preverbal understanding suggests Freud avoided venturing beneath the oedipal level, in defense against his own earlier conflicts (Meadow, 1984; Margolis, 1996; Blum, 1979; van den Berg, 1997).

While demonstrating his theory, *The Interpretation of Dreams* also serves as a vehicle permitting Freud to call himself "author." Thomas (1990) asserts that Freud's wish to publish, surpassing other writers and his own dying father, was an important factor for him, apparent in many of his dreams. Freud's (1900) interpretations of his dreams in the Botanical Monograph (p. 169), Autodidasker (p. 298), Self-Dissection (p. 452), and His Mother and the Bird Beaked Figures (p. 583) all contain references to books. The wish to write and publish is reached by way of an oedipal interpretation with competitive, ambitious aims. The publication of a book can vicariously represent a wish to be born by reproducing one's self, a child, an heir after one's death, or by defending against a wish to die. On a preoedipal level van den Berg (1997) suggests that Freud's wish to publish *The Interpretation of Dreams* is concerned with the book as the maternal body. As the specimen flower is contained within the pages of a book in his dream, the Botanical Monograph, so too does Freud long to be contained inside the body of his mother. At the same time the preoedipal mother is a destroyer. The wish to be contained within her body goes hand in hand with a wish to tear her apart (Klein, 1946).

Freud's defensive refusal to assign relevance to the mother is noteworthy in his reference to a "widowed" woman in his most famous dream, Irma's Injection, where he makes no mention of the widowed Amelia (van den Berg,1997). His disavowal of her only serves to underscore her (denied) importance. However, Freud (1900) adds another disclaimer, stating, "I will not pretend that I have completely uncovered the meaning of this dream. . . . I myself know the points from which further trains of thought could be followed" (p. 120). Freud refers to the "dream's navel" (p. 525), a place where no further interpretation can be made and where contact is made with the unknown. Publicly, he did not explore that mysterious point that may have led him to the preoedipal mother. Lacan (1954–55a), while acknowledging Freud's full development of the "function of unconscious desire," states that here Freud seems content to "present a dream which is entirely explained by the satisfaction of a desire which one cannot but call preconscious and even entirely conscious" (p. 151). Freud's writings and dreams are filled with the metaphors of reading and writing, the metaphors of the preoedipal mother. The dream takes language apart and makes use of visual images. Dreams are a regression, a return to primary process, in which "we appear not to *think* but to *experience*" (Freud, 1900, p. 50). Lacan's concept of the symbolic, the use of language, takes the dreamer away from the unconscious desire. The dreamy world of the mother is suppressed by the hard masculine world of language in the reporting of a dream (Lacan, 1954–55b).

Grinstein (1983) discusses Freud's oedipal yearnings and examines Freud's wish for recognition (for his theoretical contributions) not blame (for his secret oedipal wishes). Geltner (1984) considers the aggressive preverbal elements of Freud's wishes including an internalization of his destructive impulsivity. Spotnitz and Meadow's (1976) analysis of Irma's Injection finds that Freud had a wish not to be born but to die. When his own psyche was developing on the primitive, somatic level, before the acquisition of language, some psychic occurrence and conflict paved the way for Freud's future cancer of the jaw and palate (Meadow, 1984). The wish to destroy the preoedipal mother/self was turned inward. Freud certainly demonstrated aggressive and self-destructive wishes by destroying most of his notes and letters so that future generations would have a difficult time piecing together not only his life but his psyche (Gay, 1988). Yet the strength of his life drive and the nature of his conflict, as well as man's duality, are attested to by the fact that Freud lived to be 83. *The Interpretation of Dreams* can be seen as an expression of this duality: Freud was both destroying and recreating himself through self-analysis and the concomitant publication of a manuscript that placed him in the rank of authors.

There is no doubt that Freud had a lifelong love affair with literature. The relationship between psychoanalysis and literature may have formally begun with the publication of *The Interpretation of Dreams* though it was percolating throughout most of the nineteenth century. *The Interpretation of Dreams* was not only a theoretical account of the new science, psychoanalysis, but Freud's psychic narrative as well. Freud was influenced by the creative writers who preceded him and literature was duly influenced by Freud's (1907) publications as the analysis of literary characters in his paper, "Delusions and Dreams in Jensen's *Gradiva*," demonstrates.

Robert Louis Stevenson's Flirtation with the Unconscious

In his essay, "A Chapter on Dreams," Stevenson (1987) reports the nightmare of a college student whom he later identifies as himself. This powerful dream would provide the impetus for a fictional work that would resonate with Freud's discovery of psychic life. The dreamer, as Stevenson reveals, "passes a long day in the surgical theatre seeing monstrous malformations and the abhorred dexterity of surgeons. All night long in his wet clothes, he climbs stairs in an endless series." He repeatedly encounters "beggarly women of the street . . . muddy labourers, passing downward and all brushing against him as they pass." Eventually the dreamer finds himself "back again upon the street." At the day's beginning he is still soaking wet, "trudging to another day of monstrosities and operations" (p. 218). The dream was repetitive and Stevenson, the college student, became so obsessed with it that he could hardly separate his daily obsessions from the nightly images. Fearing insanity, he consulted a physician who prescribed a "draught" that cured him of the dream and its maddening ruminations. Shortly after having this dream,

Stevenson (1978) wrote "The Strange Case of Dr. Jekyll and Mr. Hyde," whose setting mirrors the dreamscape.

Dr. Henry Jekyll lives in quarters that are connected to his laboratory and a deserted surgical theatre. Dr. Jekyll, of course, goes on to prepare a potion or "draught" in which he transforms himself into the devilish Mr. Edward Hyde. Hyde anonymously passes people that do not recognize or acknowledge him as Dr. Jekyll. In the persona of Hyde, Jekyll attains a secret double identity. Stevenson studied engineering briefly and then law, pursuing neither profession, much to the dismay of his father, well-known builder of lighthouses. Had Stevenson been posing as a college student knowing that his fervent desire was to publish his writings?

Stevenson's literary work eerily anticipates Freud's yet-to-be-published theory of an unconscious that lies buried beneath the facade of conscious behavior. It suggests a darker side of man in which the superficial niceties of congenial "Christian" behavior are met with impulses that defy righteous loyalty, love, and charity. The ugly, narcissistic, selfish desires of humankind including impulsive desires for revenge, murder, and various wanton gratifications are explored in this gothic tale. Stevenson's Hyde embodies the respectable Dr. Jekyll's sinister side, a psychically more primitive, unrestrained version of himself.

When Jekyll is in control, he and Hyde alternately assume opposing identities, each being aware of the other. But eventually Jekyll is unable to reproduce the ameliorating potion he imbibes to restore his "good" persona. Hyde's psychic energies develop while Jekyll's life forces degenerate to a point where he cannot resurface beneath the now insuperable alter. Though the dual identities are anything but fused, they do exist in a perverse kind of harmony until Hyde refuses all attempts that would thwart his unbridled destructivity. Jekyll permanently disappears. However, Edward Hyde finds himself backed into a corner. The fugitive Hyde, wanted for his murderous atrocities, once discovered by Jekyll's friend Utterson, kills himself rather than face the gallows. In this work, Stevenson is clearly struggling with the sordid side of humanity. Stevenson is teetering on a profound understanding of the human psyche. Is man's destructivity internally or externally motivated? Stevenson is not sure. Freud will be certain.

Aggression: Internal or External?

Earlier in the story, Utterson spies Hyde from the shadows. Upon meeting Hyde for the first time he is unaware that Hyde is, in fact, his dear friend Henry Jekyll. Utterson is quite shaken by the experience and cannot stop obsessing about the hideous man. That night he dreams that Hyde is standing menacingly over Jekyll's bed in an attempt to kill him. The author's use of the dream implies that something is unconsciously communicated to Utterson. The dream is prophetic and suggests the story's impending aggression will come from outside sources. This is one explanation for the wickedness of man. Forces exist outside of him and are beyond his control. Stevenson's inclusion of the dream also hints that man may be responsible for his own follies. Intrapsychically, Utterson's/Jekyll's/Stevenson's death wishes, though oblique, are also apparent. Subtle homosexual wishes can be discernable alongside the aggression.

Psychoanalytically, Stevenson's (1978) description of Jekyll resembles a case history. Jekyll, in a written confession, speaks of the evolution of Hyde. The author focuses on the internal struggle men suffer in their choices between self-restraint and self-indulgent gratification: "All human beings are commingled out of good and evil, and Edward Hyde alone in the ranks of mankind, was pure evil" (p. 108). While Hyde was Jekyll's projection of pure evil, Hyde represents one aspect of Jekyll. Stevenson flirts with the idea that good and evil are not quite so separate. Stevenson was raised in a strict God-fearing Calvinist household where *human* evil was strictly warned against (Calder, 1980). Stevenson's Hyde captures the pleasure in human aggression.

Stevenson's fiction contains a deep appreciation of human nature. The author depicts traces of Jekyll's vice: Jekyll arranges a midnight meeting in which Hyde metamorphoses to Jekyll in the presence of his remonstrating colleague and lifetime friend Dr. Lanyon. Through a cryptic letter and various secret messengers, Jekyll sends the salts that comprise the potion to Lanyon's house. Lanyon accepts the package and waits for further instructions from Jekyll. In an almost deranged state, Hyde appears at the stroke of midnight begging for Lanyon's assistance who, though frightened, is also intrigued. Characteristic of the gothic novel, sexual imagery and innuendo permeate this scene. As Hyde enters the house, Dr. Lanyon's fear is obvious, "As I followed him [Hyde] into the bright light of the consulting-room, I kept my hand ready on my weapon. Here, at last, I had a chance of clearly seeing him" (p. 98). As if the two were meeting for a stealthy lascivious encounter, Lanyon is not quite sure of his visitor's purpose, yet he is titillated by its possibilities. Hyde, desperately wanting the chemicals, cries out for them. "And so lively was his impatience that he even laid his hand upon my arm and sought to shake me" (p. 99). Hyde sees the coveted articles in a drawer and emits a petrifying sob.

While Lanyon remains in the dark regarding the purpose of this visit, Hyde/Jekyll taunts and seduces him further. Hyde mixes the various tinctures and powders, admonishing Lanyon to make his decision as he prepares to drink the potent liquid:

And now, said he, "to settle what remains. Will you be wise? Will you be guided? Will you suffer me to take this glass in my hand, and to go forth from your house without further parley? Or had the greed of curiosity too much command of you? Think before you answer, for it shall be done as you decide. As you decide you shall be left as you were before, neither richer nor wiser, unless the sense of service rendered to a man in mortal distress may be counted as a kind of riches of the soul. Or, if you shall so prefer to choose, a new province of knowledge and new avenues of fame and power shall be laid open to you, here, in this room, upon the instant; and your sight shall be blasted by a prodigy to stagger the unbelief of Satan." (p.101)

As Lanyon agrees to see this scene to its end, Hyde/Jekyll reveals his hidden, sadistic revenge motive. Hyde/Jekyll expounds lifelong rage he has harbored toward Lanyon due to Lanyon's refutation of his scientific discoveries in medicine. Hyde, draining the glass, cries out and staggers about the room undergoing wretched, physical alteration with Lanyon's strident cry almost mimicking the orgasmic release Hyde has just displayed. When the dust settles, Henry Jekyll stands before Lanyon with no trace of Mr. Edward Hyde. Dr. Lanyon takes to his bed, will speak to no one, and in two weeks time dies, with the "knowledge" bestowed upon him by Jekyll/Hyde.

Thanatos

What is the knowledge that kills Lanyon? Is it the knowledge that man does not exist without evil? Is it the depth of Jekyll's hatred which subjects Lanyon to such a scene totally unprepared? Is it a rape? Lanyon, seduced by Hyde and aroused in the highly sexualized scene, discovers something quite contrary to what he surmised: the murder of Hyde and the rebirth of Jekyll. While Lanyon gives his permission for Hyde to continue, he has no idea to what he is consenting. Sex or aggression? In this scene, Stevenson irrevocably forges a link in which two opposing drives exist side by side. Is it this knowledge that kills Lanyon? Or is it knowledge of the existence of an unconscious, containing unknown motives? Lanyon's belief in Jekyll as a good man is destroyed by the presence of the evil Hyde within him. The unconscious was born in that scene. Lanyon, the lone witness, was scared stiff.

Lanyon's Conflict

Why does Lanyon remain silent about this knowledge, allowing it to snuff out his life? Does he feel responsible for Jekyll's criminal transformation? Does Jekyll (Stevenson) force responsibility upon Lanyon (his father) for his own misdeeds? Is the father responsible for the actions of the son? This resounds with one of the fundamental questions of nineteenth-century literature: is there a higher power in control of man's actions or is man responsible for his own conduct? Freud would eventually answer the latter question in the affirmative. Lanyon has metaphorically fallen from the Garden of Eden. He is innocent no more, having witnessed the utter degradation and destructivity of man. Lanyon, not comprehending what he has learned, is so overwhelmed that he would rather die than speak. He does, however, write in a sealed letter to be opened post mortem by the rational Mr. Utterson. Lanyon's newfound knowledge is thrust upon him. Like Narcissus at the pool, his defenses are shattered prematurely and are replaced with a desire for death. Lanyon now has living proof of the "good" Dr. Jekyll's sinister capabilities. He cannot tolerate it; he cannot survive without his defenses. So he climbs into bed and expires.

Stevenson's Dream: An Author's Conflict

Each time Hyde kills, he becomes stronger. Tasting murder, Dr. Jekyll finds it more difficult to contain Mr. Hyde. Multiple doses of the draught become necessary for Jekyll to resurface. Eventually, Hyde dominates the two aspects of the one man and leads them both inexorably towards death. At the same time, Jekyll's own aggression is surfacing. It is he who concocts and drinks the potion unleashing the diabolical Hyde. From where did Hyde come? There is only one obvious answer: supernatural forces are not responsible in this tale of switched identity and concealed criminality. Stevenson portrays the complex internal workings of an individual.

Stevenson spent most of his life suffering from the lung disease, bronchiectasis. A diagnosis of tuberculosis was never definitively confirmed. Yet Stevenson seems to have accepted that he suffered from the more fatal affliction (Woodhead, 2001). He wrote "Jekyll and Hyde" from his bed at Bournemouth, England between alarmingly bloody coughing fits (Nabokov, 1980). It is not difficult to imagine that Stevenson longed for a "draught" that might cure him of his wicked illness or some surgical procedure that would repair his hemorrhaging lungs. He and his wife Fanny traveled from one sanitorium to the next seeking new treatments. At the same time, Robert Louis Stevenson may also have experienced gratification from the drama and dependency his illness afforded him.

The dream that inspired the story reveals information concerning Stevenson's psychic life, troubled with thoughts of death. Previously supported by his wealthy father, Stevenson was already 35 when, with "Jekyll and Hyde," he finally achieved the financial and literary success he sought. Climbing the endless stairs (in Stevenson's dream) can be interpreted as symbolic of Stevenson's conscious ambition to obtain success and health. But what can be gleaned about his unconscious motives? Was living in the shadow of death seductive to a would-be writer? Is an unknown, unpublished author really alive? Although he experienced periods of good health in which he could write, he alternately suffered major, physical deteriorations. The threat of death was ever-present for Stevenson.

In his dream, Stevenson repeatedly climbs and descends a staircase, finding himself at daybreak, his clothes wet, on the street level from where he began. Dreams can be interpreted at all psychosexual stages and developmental levels. At the oedipal level, the repetitious rising and falling of the dreamer on the stairs has sexual implications (Grinstein, 1968). And the dream climaxes when the dreamer descends from the staircase, emerging from the anonymity and secretiveness of night, his clothing wet, reminiscent of the scene with Lanyon. The dreamer's ascending while lower class characters (primitive impulses) are descending characterizes the duality of the conflict: the wish to excel or to see oneself as noble, godlike, healthy, and successful is pulling against the lower, bodily urges for sex, humiliation, sickness, and death (Grinstein, 1968).

Lacking a female protagonist, "Jekyll and Hyde" is devoid of heterosexual relationships although film (Mamoulian,1931; Fleming,1941) and theater (Phillips,1997) versions have created female love interests for Jekyll and Hyde. Doctor Jekyll, Mr. Hyde, Mr. Utterson, Mr. Enfield, the murdered Sir Danvers Carew, Dr. Lanyon, and even the butler Poole are all single males. Does the absence of female characters lend added meaning to the exclusive presence of men? Is there an unconscious homosexual element in "Jekyll and Hyde?" Nabokov

(1980) suggests that Stevenson did not intend for his story to be interpreted at this level, yet he states that homosexual behavior among men in Victorian England behind the mask of propriety was commonplace. This duality was culturally accepted. Does the author's dream reveal evidence of latent homosexuality? (Mr. Utterson's dream certainly does.) Classical Freudian symbolism indicates sexual wishes associated with forbidden impulses, but not necessarily homosexual desire, in Stevenson's dream. However, latent homosexuality within the novel can be viewed as another aspect of duality and conflict, in that unconscious homosexual impulses exist universally (Freud, 1925).

Freud (1900) gives credence to the anxiety dreams of individuals who suffer from chronic heart or lung disease (p. 34) as in his own dream, Going up the Stair (Freud, 1900, p. 238), in which he is concerned with his health and heart function. Likewise, Stevenson's health is central in this dream. Is the dreamer in a cold sweat of anxiety, fearing continued professional failure (conscious reality), sexual/homosexual urges (oedipal), or madness created by the restraint and isolation of illness in life as well as a wish to escape from life into death (preoedipal)? Does Stevenson have a sexual relationship with death? Does his own aggression excite him? At the age of 22, Stevenson wrote a letter to his mother, who frequently became ill herself when Stevenson had bouts of illness as a child, about death and churchyards. She was so intensely frightened by it that she destroyed this communication from her son (Balfour, 1901). Stevenson seems to have had both conscious and unconscious fantasies concerning death throughout much of his life.

The narrow staircase image can be understood on a deeper, preverbal level as suggesting a birth canal, particularly when the dreamer finds himself at the other end at dawn, dripping wet. In a reversal of nakedness, being clothed can symbolize birth (Grinstein, 1968). Stevenson's dream suggests a conflict between life and the "descent" toward death, representing the duality of his own struggle. He has a wish to break through and pass out of this world of illness into the tension-less state of death. Yet the symbol of dawn and the continuous ascent seem to reveal the wish to continue to live and write. All of Stevenson's works prior to "Jekyll and Hyde" were unable to capture his conflict. With "Jekyll and Hyde," Stevenson was able to reach deep within himself and reveal who he was as did Freud in *The Interpretation of Dreams*. It would seem that Stevenson's resistance to writing his autobiography in the context of a novel had been resolved. The act of working through this conflict via his characters freed Stevenson as he fleetingly found success. Robert Louis Stevenson died at the age of 44 from a cerebral hemorrhage, not chronic lung disease, at the height of his literary renown.

Conclusion

In *The Interpretation of Dreams*, Freud (1900) provides "evidence" for the existence of unconscious life upon which his entire theory is constructed. Freud did not work in a vacuum. Quite the contrary, he absorbed and synthesized ideas that were present within the culture and expressed by the intuitive sensitivities of an array of writers and thinkers whom he voraciously studied. Robert Louis Stevenson is simply an example of one literary author whose work displays an uncanny resonance with Freud's ultimate findings.

REFERENCES

Aristotle (1936), *De Anima* (On the Soul), J. Henderson, ed. W. S. Hett, translator. Cambridge, MA: Harvard University Press.
———— (1941), *De Somniis* (On Dreams). R. McKeon, ed. New York: Random House.
Balfour, G. (1901), *The Life of Robert Louis Stevenson*. Vols. 1 & 2. New York: Charles Scribner's Sons.
Bion, W. (1962), *Learning from Experience*. London: Maresfield Library.
Blum, H. (1979), The prototype of preoedipal reconstruction. *Freud and His Self Analysis*. M. Kanzer & J. Glenn, eds. New York: Jason Aronson.
Calder, J. (1990), *Robert Louis Stevenson: A Life Study*. Glasgow: Richard Drew Publishing.
Cicero (2001), *De Senectute* (On Old Age); *De Amicitia* (On Friendship); *De Divinatione* (On Divination). W. A. Falconer, translator. Cambridge, MA: Harvard University Press.
Freud, S. (1900), The interpretation of dreams. *Standard Edition*. London: Hogarth Press, 4 & 5.
———— (1907), Delusion and dream in Jensen's *Gradiva*. *Standard Edition*. London: Hogarth Press, 9:7–93.
———— (1909), Family romances. *Standard Edition*. London: Hogarth Press, 9:237–241.
———— (1918[1914]) From the history of an infantile neurosis. *Standard Edition*. London: Hogarth Press, 17.
———— (1925 [1924]), An autobiographical study. *Standard Edition*. London: Hogarth Press, 20.

Gay, P. (1988), *Freud: A Life for Our Time,* New York: Norton.

Geltner, P. (1984), Reflections on Freud's dream "Irma's injection." *Modern Psychoanalysis,* 9:191–202.

Grinstein, A. (1983), *Freud's Rules of Dream Interpretation.* Madison, CT: International Universities Press.

———— (1980), *Sigmund Freud's Dreams.* New York: International Universities Press.

Hobson, J. A. (1988), *The Dreaming Brain.* New York: Basic Books.

———— (1999), The new neuropsychology of sleep: implications for psychoanalysis. *Neuro-Psychoanalysis,* 1(2):157–183.

———— (2002), *Dreaming: An Introduction to the Science of Sleep.* New York: Oxford University Press.

Hobson, J. A. & J. A. Leonard (2001), *Out of Its Mind.* Cambridge, MA: Perseus.

Hobson, J. A. & R. W. McCarley (1977), The brain as a dream state generator: an activation-synthesis hypothesis of the dream process. *The American Journal of Psychiatry,* 134:1335–1348.

Jones, E. (1961), *The Life and Work of Sigmund Freud.* L. Trilling & S. Marcus, eds. New York: Basic Books.

Jung, C. G. (1968), *Psychology and Alchemy.* Princeton, NJ: Princeton University Press.

Klein, M. (1946), Notes on some schizoid mechanisms. *The Selected Melanie Klein.* J. Mitchell, ed. New York: Free Press, 1987.

Lacan, J., (1954-55a), The dream of Irma's injection. *The Seminar of Jacques Lacan: Book II, The Ego in Freud's Theory and in the Technique of Psychoanalysis 1954–1955.* New York: Norton.

———— (1954–55b), Desire, life and death. *The Seminar of Jacques Lacan: Book II, The Ego in Freud's Theory and in the Technique of Psychoanalysis 1954–1955.* New York: Norton.

Lucretius (1968), *De Rerum Natura* (The Way Things Are). R. Humphries, translator. Bloomington, IN: Indiana University Press.

Margolis, D. (1996), *Freud and His Mother.* Northvale, NJ: Jason Aronson.

Meadow, P. W. (1984), The royal road to preverbal conflicts. *Modern Psychoanalysis,* 9:63–92.

Nabokov, V. (1980), Robert Louis Stevenson: the strange case of Dr. Jekyll and Mr. Hyde. *Lectures on Literature.* F. Bowers, ed. Orlando, FL: Harcourt Brace.

Ogden, T. (2001), *Conversations at the Frontier of Dreaming.* Northvale, NJ: Jason Aronson.

Plato (1955), *The Republic.* D. Lee, translator. London: Penguin.

Quinodoz, J. M. (2002), *Dreams That Turn Over a Page: Paradoxical Dreams in Psychoanalysis*. New York: Brunner-Routledge.

Segal, H. (1991), *Dream, Phantasy and Art*. E. Bott Spillius, ed. New York: Routledge.

Sharpe, E. F. (1937), *Dream Analysis*. London: Hogarth Press.

Solms, M. (1995), New findings on the neurological organization of dreaming: implications for psychoanalysis. *The Psychoanalytic Quarterly*, 64:43–67.

————— (1997), *The Neuropsychology of Dreams: A Clinico-Anatomical Study*. Mahwah, NJ: Lawrence Erlbaum Associates.

————— (1999), The new neuropsychology of sleep: commentary. *Neuro-Psychoanalysis*, 1(2):83–195.

Spotnitz, H. & P. W. Meadow (1976), Dreams: the royal road to preoedipal conflicts. *Treatment of the Narcissistic Neuroses*. New York: MCAPS.

Stevenson, R. L. (1978), *The Strange Case of Dr. Jekyll and Mr. Hyde*. New York: Penguin.

————— (1979), *Dr. Jekyll and Mr. Hyde and Other Stories*. New York: Penguin.

————— (1987), *The Lantern-Bearers and Other Essays*. J. Treglown, ed. New York: Cooper Square Press.

————— (1995), *Dr. Jekyll and Mr. Hyde and Other Stories*. New York: Barnes and Noble.

Thomas, R. (1990), *Dreams of Authority*. Ithaca, NY: Cornell University Press.

van de Castle, R. L. (1994), *Our Dreaming Mind*. New York: Ballantine Books.

van den Berg, S., (1997), Reading the object: Freud's dreams. PSYART: *A Hyperlink Journal for Psychological Study of the Arts*.

Winson, J. (1985) *Brain & Psyche: The Biology of the Unconscious*. New York: Random House.

————— (1990), The meaning of dreams. *Scientific American*. August 31.

Wolff, W. (1952), *The Dream: Mirror of Conscience*. New York: Grune & Stratton

Woodhead, R. (2001), *The Strange Case of R. L. Stevenson*. Edinburgh: Luath Press.

Woods, R. L. & H. B. Greenhouse, eds. (1974), *The New World of Dreams: An Anthology*. New York: Macmillan

6735 Ridge Boulevard
Brooklyn, NY 11220
Barbdamato@aol.com

Infandum: Oral-Sadistic Imagery in Dante's *Inferno*, Canto XXXIII

CHRISTIAN TALBOT

An episode of cannibalism from Dante's Inferno *is examined in order to explore the psychodynamics of oral sadism. The "case study" illustrates the libidinal and aggressive aims of the protagonist's oral sadism, especially as a defense against an intolerable feeling of impotence and a maladaptive discharge of destructive aggression. Ultimately the episode reveals that literal cannibalism can be conceived of as the "sin" of destructive narcissism while verbal communion with the Other can be thought of as the "virtue" of object-relatedness.*

Some things don't get talked about. In psychoanalysis, we call that which keeps something unspoken a resistance. But resistance is idiosyncratic. What one person can say quite comfortably and openly may cause another person to turn red with embarrassment or stony with anger, perhaps leaving them totally speechless. And while psychoanalysis is most famously known as "the talking cure," there are other symbolic communications equally important to the process of interpretation. So the analyst understands the patient only when he properly interprets the patient's unconscious signs. Just as much as the words themselves, interpreting the *resistance* to speaking, or the even more powerful resistance, that which blocks unconscious thoughts from developing into words, stands out as one of the two key tasks of the analyst.[1]

In Latin, the word *infans* means "speechless" or "unable to speak." The prefix *in* means "un" and *fari* means "to speak"; it is not coincidental that our word "infant" describes the period of human develop-

[1] The other being the interpretation of transference.

ment before speech develops. More instructive is the participle of this word: *infandum*, not only "unspeakable," but also "unnatural" or "abominable." We can begin to see why there are such powerful resistances to putting into words our most primitive impulses and wishes since from a psychoanalytic point of view such impulses originate in the unconscious mental life of the infant.

In an essay titled "The Beast in the Nursery," the British psychoanalyst Adam Phillips (1998) comments, "Language is a cure for infancy; but children take to it with varying degrees of eagerness. . . . Nothing terrorizes people more in our culture than the refusal of food and the refusal of words" (p. 48). His words have an eerie resonance with the penultimate, horrific episode of Dante's *Inferno*: the tale of Count Ugolino, who allegedly cannibalized his children.

Singleton (1970), quoting Filippo Villani's 1847 *Illustrated Lives of Famous Florentines*, provides the most complete concise account of Ugolino's tragic tale. The count, having betrayed his home city of Pisa in a moment of apparently characteristic opportunism, was himself betrayed by his partner-in-crime, Archbishop Ruggieri. As a punishment, Ugolino and his four sons[2] were locked in a tower to starve to death. When the bodies were removed, they showed signs of having been bitten and eaten. While contemporary commentators believe this to have been the work of rats, Dante implies that Ugolino cannibalized his children to prolong his life.

This penultimate episode in Dante's *Inferno*, the famous Ugolino passage, reveals the role of libidinal and aggressive impulses in an act of cannibalism. Symbolic communications, parapraxis, a dream, and an enactment bring to light the unconscious origins and meanings of the cannibalistic behavior of the main character, Ugolino. Ultimately, the preponderance of oral-libidinal and oral-sadistic imagery demonstrates that the narcissistic defense, in the form of rageful silence and a somatic attack, cannot withstand an excessive quotient of aggression when it is coupled with a desire to restore a lost, libidinal object.

Review of the Literature

A sampling of the psychoanalytic literature reveals two major understandings of the concept of oral sadism: oral sadism as an expression of

---

[2]In real life, Ugolino was imprisoned with two of his sons and two grandsons, all of whom were either teenagers or adults. Dante manipulates these facts not only to provide an even more tragic picture, but also to underscore the innocence of children with the wickedness of men.

a libidinal impulse and as an expression of an aggressive impulse. In each case, object relations plays a secondary role to the drives.

Freud was the first to discuss orality. His understanding, which apparently he never revised, rests upon his libido theory. In "Three Essays on the Theory of Sexuality," Freud (1905) argues that orality, even when it bears the appearance of sadism, has the libidinal aim of incorporation. Freud (1913) advances this argument again in "Totem and Taboo" where he writes, "By incorporating parts of a person's body through the act of eating, one at the same time acquires the qualities possessed by him" (p. 82). One cannot deny that such an act also provides an outlet for aggression in the use of the mouth as a destructive device, but as D'Amato (2002) points out, "The *primary* purpose is to release aggression via oral incorporation" (p. 153, italics added). McDougall (1995) concurs: "There is little doubt that such incorporative fantasies in which one becomes the other by eating the person or the part of the person that is desired, represent archaic libidinal longings" (p. 135). This position places her squarely in line with Freud, who also believed that acts of oral sadism represent early (for McDougall "archaic") strivings on the part of the infant to bring together itself with some desired object—presumably the breast. Freeman and Freeman (1992) support the idea of oral-sadism as a representation of a libidinal rather than an aggressive urge by pointing out that Freud conceived of sadism as a component instinct requiring an object. Since the infant's psyche is, presumably, at a pre-object level, infantile sadism as an expression of aggression, per se, would be impossible.[3]

Though concurring that oral-sadistic behavior suggests a desire to incorporate the object, Abraham (1924) argues that revenge also plays a role in oral sadism. He writes that "The process of introjection in the melancholic . . . is based on . . . a severe conflict of ambivalent feelings, from which he can only escape by turning against himself the hostility he originally felt towards his object" (p. 438). In this scenario, one deals with deeply ambivalent feelings by holding on to the lost object (and the source of the melancholy) in order to attack and, presumably, destroy it, thereby eliminating the conflict. Practically speaking, this means that after taking in the object through some orally sadistic method, the patient turns the aggression, in the form of melancholy, against the self since that is where the object now resides. This marks a departure from Freud's notion that oral sadism has incorporation as its

[3]It still remains a mystery why Freud did not revise his notion of oral sadism as expressed in cannibalism after he (1920) posited a separate "death drive."

primary aim; here, Abraham seems to suggest that aggression—in the form of a desire for revenge[4]—represents the underlying impulse. It follows, then, that "in the biting stage of the oral phase the individual incorporates the object in himself and in so doing destroys it" (p. 451). In other words, the libidinal aim is subordinate to the aggressive aim.

Klein (1930, 1956) adopts Abraham's notion that oral sadism serves a destructive as well as libidinal aim. But whereas Abraham conceives of the aggressive component as potentially originating in childhood, Klein situates the emergence of the precipitating ambivalence at a more archaic stage of development. As the Freeman and Freeman (1992) point out, "For Klein a part object relationship (partial incorporation) exists from birth" (p. 343); therefore, Klein theorized that such acts of aggression, which she "regarded as derivatives of the death instinct" (p. 343), can emerge at birth.[5] Klein (1930) wrote about the dual motivations of the oral-sadistic infant, in which she defines the essentially destructive aspect of the infant's introjecting desired parts of the mother (which she terms "greed") and the obviously destructive extrojection (which she terms "envy") involved in wishing to destroy the good object:

> At the unconscious level, [the infant's] greed aims primarily at scooping out, sucking dry and devouring the breast, that is to say, its aim is destructive introjection, whereas [the infant's] envy not only aims at robbing in this way, but also at putting badness, primarily bad excrements and bad parts of the self, into the mother—first of all into her breast—in order to spoil and destroy her. (p. 152)

Oral sadism, for Klein, has an unmistakably aggressive aim, even when it seeks to take something away from the breast, hence Klein's use of the term "*destructive* introjection."

Finally, Spotnitz and Meadow (1995) synthesize the Freudian and Kleinian views about the roles of libido and aggression in oral sadism by arguing that the same mechanism active in the impulse to attack the object can also be used to attack the self in a sacrificial manner, culminating in the schizophrenic defense:

> In one of the earliest attempts to explain the withdrawal from objects, Klein (1930) attributed this withdrawal to the ego's "exaggerated and premature defense against sadism, beginning in the first few months of

---

[4]Abraham (1924) writes, "The teeth are the only organs [small children] possess that are sufficiently hard to be able to injure objects around them" (p. 451).

[5]Contrary to Freud's belief that there could be no such thing as infantile sadism.

life." The turning of destructive impulses against the object, which is first expressed in fantasied oral-sadistic attacks on the mother's breast . . . leads to the development of mechanisms regarded as tremendously important for the development of [schizophrenia]. (p. 6)

For Spotnitz and Meadow, when the individual's aggression becomes overpowering, he has two choices: he may turn it against the environment or against himself. In its most radical and severe form, the latter option manifests itself as the schizophrenic reaction, in which the ego is fragmented by unmanageable aggression (Spotnitz, 2004).

The academic literature often focuses on the question of whether Ugolino actually cannibalized his sons. In one sense, this is a moot question for the purposes of this essay since so much other oral-sadistic imagery abounds in the episode. On the other hand, what is at stake in such a debate is an understanding of what Ugolino might have been attempting to do by cannibalizing his sons. Herzman (1980) and Chiarenza (1989) both argue persuasively for cannibalism, while Mandelbaum (1981) and Ahern (1998) are not necessarily convinced by this interpretation. Freccero (1986), however, argues most convincingly for the anthropophagic interpretation in his classic essay "Bestial Sign and Bread of Angels." Singleton (1970), Freccero's one-time mentor, was completely dismissive[6] of such a notion; Hollander (2000) concurs with Singleton.

Canto XXXIII

A brief description of the entire *Divine Comedy* as well as the narrative and thematic structure of *Inferno* seems appropriate as a context for understanding the particular case of Ugolino. Dante's *Divine Comedy* is a three-part epic poem consisting of three *cantiche*, or "books": *Inferno, Purgatorio,* and *Paradiso*. In the simplest sense, the poem depicts the descent through Hell, then the ascent up the mountain of Purgatory by Dante and the great Latin poet Virgil, and concludes with

[6]Singleton (1970) says, "Some commentators have held the curious view that by this last line of Ugolino's narrative Dante meant to imply that the count, in the extremity of starvation, did actually attempt to prolong his life by feeding upon the bodies of his sons. . . . But such a view of the meaning here is hardly worth a serious rebuttal" (p. 617). It is perhaps an example of parapraxis that Singleton rationalizes his failure to speak about cannibalism by indicating that such a notion is "hardly worth serious rebuttal"; such a phrase implies the very quality of *infandum* that Freccero (1986) identifies at work in the episode.

Dante's movement through the Empyrean—that is, Heaven—accompanied by Beatrice, once his earthly love, now an archon of divine love. Some readers are content to read all three books as a representation of an actual spiritual experience of Dante's. Most, however, agree that the poem serves as an allegory for the human experience of the journey[7] through the various stages of life, bounded by sin and salvation at each turn.[8]

Inferno, like the other two books of the poem, follows a spiral structure that reflects an ever-deepening journey. Dante and Virgil enter the gates of Hell to discover separate rings, or circles, whose punishments correspond to the primary sins of their occupants. For example, the second circle of Hell contains the "Lustful," individuals whose sensual desires overpowered them and others; the seventh circle, by contrast, contains the "Violent"—murderers and tyrants. Each descending circle shrinks in diameter, but the farther down Dante travels, the deeper each ring seems to become. At the very bottom of Hell, in the ninth circle, rather than the "fire and brimstone" made famous in Joyce's *Portrait of the Artist as a Young Man*, Dante encounters a vast lake of ice, in which the "Traitorous" (to their benefactors) are frozen. This is where we find Ugolino.

A last word about the thematic structure of *Inferno* is in order. Commentators have made frequent note of Dante's use of *contrapasso* —literally "counter-suffering"—to punish the various sinners. While the suffering for each sinner is relative to the sins for which they have been damned—that is, the punishments become progressively more painful and harrowing as Dante descends—they are, for each sinner, absolute, inasmuch as each sin is punished by its perfect correlative. So, for example, Francesca di Rimini, an adulteress, is punished for her excessive lust by suffering the eternal buffeting of a storm. The commission of the sin—uncontrollable lust—is transformed into the suffering of a metaphor for that same sin—the uncontrollable storm. As the gates of Hell tell Dante, "Justice" and "the Highest Wisdom" (III.4, 6) are as the architects for Hell.

With these thoughts in mind, let us turn to the final lines of Canto XXXII, which abounds with cannibalistic imagery. Here, Dante

[7]The first line of the poem reads:
When I had journeyed half of our life's way
I found myself within a shadowed forest
for I had lost the path that does not stray

[8]Helen Luke's (1989) *Dark Wood to White Rose: Journey and Transformation in Dante's Divine Comedy* stands out as the only full-length psychological treatment of the entire poem. She reads Dante's journey through the lens of Jungian psychology.

encounters Ugolino and his mortal enemy Archbishop Ruggieri in Hell's ninth and lowest circle. Together in a lake of ice, Ugolino and Ruggieri are permanently frozen together, literally and figuratively, in the hideous act of anthropophagy: "I saw two shades frozen in one hole,/so that one's head served as the other's cap;/and just as he who's hungry chews his bread,/one sinner dug his teeth into the other/right at the place where brain is joined to nape" (XXXII, 125–129). Dante further compares (130-131) Ugolino to Tydeus, one of the Seven against Thebes, and Ruggieri to Menalippus, Tydeus's enemy and vanquisher. According to Statius's account in the *Thebaid*, Tydeus cannibalizes the dead Menalippus in a moment of rage before dying himself. All told, there are six references to eating or the mouth[9] in the final 12 lines of Canto XXXII.

Not surprisingly, in the very first line of Canto XXXIII, in which he recounts Ugolino's tale, Dante identifies Ugolino by his mouth: "La bocca sollevò dal fiero pasto/quel peccator," in the Italian. Mandelbaum (1981) translates the line in typical English syntax with the subject coming at the beginning of the sentence: "That sinner raised his mouth from his fierce meal." But Dante begins the first line of the canto with "La bocca"—the mouth—and this poetic rearrangement of the syntax in the Italian intensifies our identification of Ugolino with his mouth, the agent of the most radical form of oral sadism: cannibalism. Ugolino then goes on to wipe his mouth and lips on the hair of his enemy in grotesque mockery of good table manners.

In order to tell his tale, Ugolino claims that he must "renew despairing pain" (XXXIII.4–5). But while Ugolino is not inclined to speak about his final moments on earth, the opportunity for further revenge motivates him: "But if my words are the seeds from which the fruit/is infamy for this betrayer whom/I gnaw, you'll see me speak and weep at once" (7–8). Here we see the first verbalization of Ugolino's hatred for Ruggieri, which has hitherto found expression only in his silent, savage attack on the flesh of the Archbishop's neck and brains.

The story of Ugolino's imprisonment and death is fairly short. Having accused Ugolino of betraying the state of Pisa, Ruggieri locks up Ugolino and his four sons in the Eagles' Tower—which, Ugolino points out, "now, through me, is called the Hunger Tower" (23)—to starve them to death.

After several nights, Ugolino tells Dante that he "dreamed that bad dream/which rent the curtain of the future for me" (26–27). In his dream, a man appears to Ugolino as "lord and master" who "hunted down the

---

[9]"Chews his bread," "dug his teeth," "gnawed the temples," chewed the skull," "on whom you feed," and "if that with which I speak does not dry up" (XXXII, 127-139).

wolf and its young whelps . . . /But after a brief course, it seemed to me that both the father and the sons were weary; I seemed to see their flanks torn by sharp fangs" (28–36). In the very next line, Ugolino recalls, "When I awoke at daybreak, I could hear/my sons, who were together with me there,/weeping within their sleep, asking for bread" (37–38).

When the time for feeding arrives, "each, because of what he'd dreamed, was anxious" (45). At that moment, the door to the tower is nailed shut, and Ugolino falls silent: "without a word,/I looked into the faces of my sons./I did not weep; within, I turned to stone" (47–49). He remains silent, even as his children question him, but after another day without food, Ugolino says, "I saw,/reflected in four faces, my own gaze,/[and] out of my grief, I bit at both my hands" (56–58). His children, interpreting this gesture as a sign of hunger rather than grief or rage, offer themselves as food: "Father,/it would be far less painful for us if/you ate of us" (60–62). Ugolino responds quickly but wordlessly: "Then I grew calm, to keep them from more sadness;/through that day and the next, we all were silent" (64–65). Soon, Gaddo, Ugolino's fourth son, cries out, "Father, why do you not help me?" but the Count refuses to break his silence and Gaddo dies there at his feet. One by one, then, his sons die over the next two days. Ugolino himself goes blind from starvation, then "started groping over each;/and after they were dead, I called them for/two days" (73–74). Finally, Ugolino says, "fasting had more force than grief" (75).

While the Ugolino episode is the penultimate narrative moment of Dante's *Inferno*, it represents the most emotionally dramatic point of the poem; the final scene, in which Virgil and Dante see Lucifer lodged in the center of the Earth, is in many ways anticlimactic. Clearly, what lends the Ugolino episode its resonance is the unspeakable horror of the cannibalism of innocent children.

Cantos XXXII and XXXIII raise the following questions about Ugolino's oral sadism: What does he wish to destroy? What does he wish to preserve? To what extent does the unspeakable nature of his act play a role in the depiction of his character structure?

Oral Sadism: The Role of Destructive Aggression

Ugolino's ravenous, crazed attack on the flesh of Ruggieri incarnates the destructive aggression underlying Ugolino's hatred of his enemy. Kernberg (1995) is most instructive in describing this phenomenon:

Hatred is a complex, structured derivative of the affect rage that expresses several wishes: to destroy a bad object, to make it suffer, and to control it. In contrast to the acute, transitory, and disruptive quality of rage,
it is a chronic, stable, usually characterologically anchored or structured
affect. The object relationship framing this affect expresses concretely
the desire to destroy or dominate the object. (p. 2)

Dante recognizes this controlling, sadistic dimension when he says to
Ugolino, "O you who show, with such a bestial sign/your hatred for the
one on whom you feed,/tell me the cause" (XXXII.133–135).
Furthermore, when Kernberg speaks about the structured quality of
rage, he is referring to object constancy. In this case, it would be entirely unsatisfying for Ruggieri to disappear after Ugolino cannibalizes
him; in order for the revenge to be effective, the archbishop needs to
remain a stable, constant presence. In this way, Ugolino can act out his
wish to both control and destroy the hated object. At the same time,
however, the constancy of that object serves as a torturous reminder to
Ugolino of the hideous starvation and death that he and his sons were
forced to endure.

This splitting also reveals the role of projection as an essential key to
the hatred that Ugolino feels for Ruggieri. His enemy not only serves
as the object of quite justifiable hatred for imprisoning Ugolino and his
sons; Ruggieri also conveniently serves as a receptacle for the hated,
split-off parts of himself. Instead of feeling guilt for his betrayal of
Pisa, Ugolino can lay the blame on Ruggieri; instead of recalling with
appropriate humility his imprisonment and inability to save himself or
his sons, Ugolino can attack Ruggieri, who is himself imprisoned in a
lake of ice and incapable of defending himself. To be sure, Dante chore-
ographs both sinners' punishments to reflect the *contrapasso* of Divine
Justice.[10] But the arrangement also subtly corresponds to the psychic
process of projection, especially as it serves as a function of splitting.

Ugolino's response to Dante's request to tell his tale further reveals
the role of hatred in Ugolino's oral-sadistic attack. First, he wipes his
mouth and lips on Ruggieri's hair in an unconscious travesty of table
manners: There is no reason to display such good manners when cannibalizing someone. If a travesty is defined as "an absurd or grotesque
misrepresentation" (*Concise Oxford English Dictionary*, 2002) then
this gesture seems to evince a certain degree of splitting in Ugolino:
Ruggieri represents the bad object which needs to be controlled and
destroyed (as per Kernberg), and so Ugolino treats the head as if it were
nothing more than a napkin. At the same time, Ugolino preserves him-

---

[10]Before he enters Hell, Dante reads on the Gates: "Justice urged on my high maker" (III. 4).

self as the good object by disguising his heinous crime of cannibalism with his fastidious gesture.

When Ugolino moves from the physical to the verbal as he seeks a more powerful modality for revenge, he stops cannibalizing Ruggieri and instead begins to savor the opportunity to defame his enemy. "[I]f my words are the seeds from which the fruit/is infamy for this betrayer whom/I gnaw, you'll see me speak and weep at once" (XXXIII.7–8), Ugolino tells Dante. The prospect of further destroying[11] his enemy excites Ugolino, so much so that he claims now to be able to endure the "despairing grief" which has previously kept him silent. As Abraham (1924) reminds us, "The component instinct of sadism, as it exists in the infantile libido, also shows us two opposite, pleasurable tendencies at work. One of these tendencies is to *destroy* the object (or the external world); the other is to control it" (p. 428). By incorporating Ruggieri through cannibalism, Ugolino may both destroy his enemy and control him. This he can accomplish through his exclusive ability to retell their shared story; whereas his teeth had been doing the job, now his words take over. We see this first in Ugolino's declaration, "You are to know I *was* Count Ugolino,/and this one is Archbishop Ruggieri" (13–14, emphasis added). Clearly, Ugolino wants to disavow his former traitorous self, evident in his use of the past tense, while his enemy must remain lodged in an eternal present tense. In using such a rhetorical device to establish his supremacy over his enemy, Ugolino initiates another, more refined modality of oral-sadistic revenge. This manipulation of words to defame Ruggieri suggests Ugolino's need for control of the hated object that Abraham and Kernberg cite in cases of oral-sadistic and rageful characters.

However, the key to Ugolino's aggressive oral-sadistic character lies, unsurprisingly, in the dream he has before his son's deaths. He establishes the oral-sadistic impulse early when he states that he "dreamed that bad dream/which rent the curtain of the future for me" (26–27). The word "rent" echoes the phrasing of line 36, in which Ugolino describes the young wolves being "torn by sharp fangs." But Ugolino envisions someone else to be the perpetrator, a "lord and master" who sends his own hounds to hunt down and tear apart the family of wolves. Ugolino fails to recognize the possibility that he himself may be the "lord and master," the powerful father-figure who possesses the urge to devour "the father and the sons [who] were weary" (35). This disavowal of his role in the destruction of his children highlights what Spotnitz and Meadow (1995) identify as the key to understanding the narcissistic

[11]With words—another form of oral sadism.

dimension of dreams. They refer to Freud's understanding (1900) that dreams "represent all within us that has not been organized in language" (p. 96). From this point of view, the aggression may be so threatening to his self-image as the good (and powerful) father that it prevents the organization of Ugolino's awareness of his murderous impulses.

Moreover, Spotnitz and Meadow (1995) go on to say that dreams "disguise the emotional experiences of the first three years of life": "[I]f we could only get in touch with the wishes that hide within the depths of the unconscious, we'd find out that people aren't really evil, but that this material comes from a period of life when we are helpless and dependent and feel that we cannot cope with the experience we are having" (p. 96). Ugolino has been imprisoned, a situation that stirs within him perhaps a helplessness similar to that of infancy, and finds himself overwhelmed by his drives. We can read the dream, then, as an expression of a preverbal reenactment. One might hypothesize that the terrifying feeling of weakness that he and his sons experience echoes "the emotional experiences of the first three years of life," as Spotnitz and Meadow (1995) note. In order to compensate for this emotional vulnerability, embodied in the already "weary" wolves, Ugolino perhaps adopts an opposite persona—a kind of reaction formation—by refashioning himself as "lord and master," terms that connote power and agency. More importantly, this dominating[12] figure in Ugolino's dream employs his "lean and keen/and practiced hounds" (31–32) to bite into the vulnerable flesh of the wolves, much as Ugolino himself will employ his teeth in a canine fashion: When Ugolino had finished his tale, "he gripped [Ruggieri's] sad skull in his teeth,/which, like a dog's, were strong down to the bone" (78–79). It is symptomatic of his deep ambivalence that in reflecting on his dream, Ugolino consciously disavows his role as the aggressor while unconsciously he attacks not only his children, but himself.

Freccero (1986) alludes to an analogous interpretation of Ugolino as the "lord and master" when he claims, "[Ugolino] infers from this incident in his dream no more than can be learned from any of the prophecies in hell: that is, that he and his children will die" (pp. 158–159). Kernberg (1995), who argues that excessively powerful aggression can actually neutralize the mind's ability to symbolize, validates Freccero's hypothesis that "Ugolino's failure is an inability to interpret the Christian hope contained in the words of his children" (p. 158). Kernberg further substantiates Freccero's position through his assertion that overly aggressive personalities lack "subliminatory channeling" (p.

[12]It is interesting to note that the English word "dominate" comes from the Latin dominus, meaning "lord." It provides the same root as the Italian word "donno" that Dante uses for "lord."

3); in other words, such individuals cannot sublimate or adaptively transform (into a symbolic alternative) their aggression. This may explain why, for Freccero, Ugolino cannot think about his dream or his children's later requests for contact except in the most literal—i.e., cannibalistic—way. But whereas Freccero's understanding is predicated on Ugolino's inability to understand the Christological significance—the spiritual significance—of his relationship with his sons, a psychoanalytic interpretation offers further evidence of his underlying oral-sadistic character. In addition to serving as a kind of reaction formation against the infantile state of vulnerability, the thinly veiled cannibalism in the dream may also shed light on Ugolino's unconscious wish to attack the symbols of innocence and weakness—both his sons and himself[13]—which are the causes of this immediate feeling of helplessness. Though Ugolino does not appear consciously to blame his sons for increasing his agony by reminding him of his paternal responsibility to them, the dream further reveals Ugolino's rage at his children and his own weak self. It is not unreasonable to suspect that Ugolino suffers his own impotence more keenly through his inability to help his sons, who cry out to him for help.[14] So it may be that by killing the children and the weak version of himself in his mind, he relieves his pent-up rage at having to bear the burden of responsibility for their suffering. This points, too, to Ugolino's intensely narcissistic character—once more validated in Spotnitz and Meadow's (1995) remarks on dream interpretation—since he seems incapable of sufficiently differentiating himself from his sons, who themselves serve as mirrors for his feeble self.

The attack on the weak version of himself reflected in such a reading of the dream continues in his waking self-attacks. These modified forms of the schizophrenic reaction appear to protect Ugolino from consciously recognizing his desire to obliterate the internalized objects that are causing his added suffering since he directs his rage at himself, first by shutting himself up, and later by biting his own hand. At the moment that Ugolino and his sons realize that the tower door is being nailed shut for good, Ugolino responds congruently by "nailing shut" his mouth: "without a word,/I looked into the faces of my sons./I did not weep; within, I turned to stone" (47–49). In an ironic twist, Ugolino's oral sadism expresses itself not through the use of his mouth, but through his refusal to use his mouth. Instead of using the mouth to direct his attack outward—say, by shouting out invective against

[13]Dante writes, "Both the father and the sons were weary;/I seemed to see their flanks torn by sharp fangs" (35–36).

[14]"Father, you look so. . . . What is wrong with you," asks Anselmuccio, while Gaddo cries out, "Father why do you not help me?" (51, 69).

Ruggieri, or even simply by crying out—Ugolino turns his aggression inward, making himself stony with silence.[15]

Here we see further signs of what Kernberg (1995) claims is the disorganizing power of excessive aggression: "At times, the intensity of hatred is such that it results in a primitive effort of denial of hatred by means of the destruction of all awareness of the affect" (p. 3). Ugolino appears, in this moment, to kill off his feelings because he perceives them as too threateningly hateful for his children to tolerate. However, as a prototype of the schizophrenic defense, such a strategy is doomed to failure since in order to spare his children his aggression, Ugolino must attack himself instead. He goes a step further when, after seeing "reflected in four faces . . . my own gaze" (57), Ugolino "bit at both my hands . . . out of my grief" (58). He can only direct his rage, which pushes harder and harder for release, against his own body. Finally, "to keep them from more sadness" (64), Ugolino makes himself calm down, presumably another indication of the flattening of affect that Kernberg cites in cases of overwhelming aggression. But nowhere is such an obliteration of affect so evident as in Dante's description of Ugolino after his last words, at which point he grips Ruggieri's head and renews his cannibalistic attack "with eyes awry," further comparing him to a dog. Not only is the affect destroyed here, but also Ugolino's essential human qualities, which give way to an almost literal dehumanization as he devolves into a dog-like state.

The schizophrenic defense, even when expressed only partially, clearly cannot successfully bind Ugolino's aggression, which Dante underscores by ironizing the familial relationships. This irony highlights the destructive power of Ugolino's envy: We see the children behaving like adults in their attempts to console a despairing father, while Ugolino behaves childishly[16] in his refusal to talk. Kernberg (1995) explains that primitive envy may operate in such a situation since we can define envy as "the need to spoil and destroy the object that is also needed for survival and, in the end, the object of love" (p. 2). In his refusal to talk to his sons, Ugolino seems symbolically to say, "I may need you, but I hate you for being good and for being innocent, and since I can't be those things myself, I will spite you by spiting myself." Eventually, in cannibalizing them, Ugolino takes the final step in destroying these good objects out of envy.

[15]Of course, at the same time, Ugolino's silence must also be understood as a kind of aggression against his tearful and hungry children, who naturally look to their father for help. Instead of loving words, nothing but "stony silence" greets them.

[16]One might even say as an infant since he is, literally *infans*—"without speech."

Oral Sadism: Introjection, Preservation, and Melancholy

Yet we should not read his oral sadism solely as expression of unadulterated aggression since implicit in Ugolino's behavior is the act of incorporation.[17] By ingesting[18] them, Ugolino may also believe that he is taking in their attendant goodness and innocence as well as enabling himself to mourn them as (literally) internalized objects. Of course, the irony—as everywhere in *Inferno*—is that Ugolino is the cause of the "loss of object" (Abraham, 1924), which occasions melancholy or depression since Ugolino is responsible for killing them off through his silence. But this same irony may help explain why Ugolino has such a powerful need to introject his children: Melancholy serves as an unconscious rationalization for the depressed person to attack himself over feelings of guilt—in this case, Ugolino's awareness that he has abused his sons. Abraham (1924) provides an extraordinary dream in support of his thesis about the incorporative aim of oral sadism and the role this incorporation plays in the formation of melancholic depressions. One of his patients, who was suffering from a melancholic depression after the death of his wife, developed a free association to a cannibalistic dream. This association in turn unlocked for Abraham the method by which oral sadism enables the melancholic to preserve the good object and thereby mourn it. Abraham reports the following observation:

> Consuming the flesh of the dead wife is made equivalent to restoring her to life. . . . Now Freud has shown that by introjecting the lost object the melancholiac does indeed recall it to life: he sets it up in his ego. . . . The process of mourning thus brings with it the consolation: "My loved object is not gone, for now I carry it within myself and can never lose it." (pp. 436–437)

Freccero (1986) corroborates this idea of orally incorporating the other in order to preserve its goodness by referencing the Eucharist, again that symbol of cannibalism remade into salvation through what the psychoanalyst might call an act of "holy sublimation": "In the seventh book of the *Confessions*, the voice of God says to Augustine, 'I am the food of grown men; grow, and thou shalt feed upon me; nor shalt thou convert me, like the food of thy flesh into thee, but thou shalt be converted into me'" (pp. 163–164). In Freccero's estimation, the act of

---

[17]"Incorporate" can be translated, literally, as "to take into the body." But there is also something of a pun involved: We may alternately think of it as "taking a body in."

[18]As Abraham (1924) writes, "The process of introjection has the character of a physical incorporation by way of the mouth" (p. 435).

Communion—of consuming the Eucharist, which for Catholics *literally* becomes the flesh of Christ[19]—enables the individual to achieve "union with Christ by love"; put another way, "a worthy Communion is to a certain extent a foretaste of heaven, in fact the anticipation and pledge of our future union with God" (newadvent.com). This is made possible through the incorporation (literally, as in Ugolino's case) of the all-good object of Jesus Christ.

In the same way, Ugolino seems to make a last ditch effort to internalize the good objects of his children before he dies so that he may always carry them around with him, in spite of his (apparently) unconscious rage towards them. Abraham (1924) explains this contradiction by citing the ambivalence underlying melancholia: "The process of introjection in the melancholiac . . . is based on a radical disturbance of his libidinal relations to his object. It rests on a severe conflict of ambivalent feelings, from which he can only escape by turning against himself [in the form of depression] the hostility he originally felt towards his object" (p. 438).

Such ambivalence compensates for the aggressive quality of Ugolino's oral sadism towards his children—embodied in the violent act of cannibalism—by demonstrating that it has a libidinal aim—incorporation of the good object, with the end result that Ugolino feels intense suffering when he recalls them. Ugolino takes great care to remind Dante of this "despair" on three[20] separate occasions. Moreover, Ugolino's cannibalism of Ruggieri provides him with an external object towards whom he can direct his conscious hatred. This might further enable him to preserve his internalized good objects since he would then only have to experience, consciously, the grief that accompanies his ambivalence when Dante persuades him to speak about his betrayal of his children.

Finally, Abraham (1924) cites Róheim, who commented[21] that "necrophagia . . . makes it very probable that in their archaic form

[19]According to the Catholic Encyclopedia, "When, therefore, He Who is All Truth and All Powers said of the bread: 'This is my body,' the bread became, through the utterance of these words, the Body of Christ; consequently, on the completion of the sentence the substance of bread was no longer present, but the Body of Christ under the outward appearance of bread. Hence the bread must have become the Body of Christ, i.e., the former must have been converted into the latter" (www.newadvent.org/cathen/0557ahtm#3).

[20]"You want me to renew/despairing pain that presses at my heart," he tells Dante when he first speaks (4–5). After telling his dream, he says, "You would be cruel indeed if, thinking what/my heart foresaw, you don't already grieve" (40–41). Finally he tells Dante, "I saw,/reflected in four faces, my own gaze,/[and] out of grief I bit at both my hands" (57–58). It is interesting that the "grief" is dispelled—momentarily—when he cannibalizes his children. "Then fasting had more strength than grief," he tells Dante, before he returns to gnawing on Ruggieri's skull.

[21]Psycho-Analytical Congress, 1922.

mourning rites consisted in the eating of the dead person" (p. 444). Such a notion not only is consistent with the imagery in the Ugolino episode that suggests the Eucharist; it also explains in a direct way the meaning behind Ugolino's treatment of his children upon their deaths: The cannibalism serves as a mourning ritual.

Cannibalism: Infandum

It is not my intention to reiterate the many arguments that members of the academy have put forward to argue for cannibalism in XXXIII.75. For the most compelling of these arguments, I would direct the reader to Freccero's (1986) landmark essay, "Bestial Sign and Bread of Angels." However, psychoanalysis—which to my knowledge academics have never formally used to support such an interpretation—seems to offer a different kind of evidence. Using the concepts of resistance and countertransference, I propose to offer some insight into the unconscious and symbolic communications from Ugolino that substantiate an interpretation consistent with Freccero, et alia.

Moore and Fine (1990) define resistances as: "attitudes, verbalizations, and actions that prevent the awareness of a perception, idea, memory, feeling, or a complex of such elements that might establish a connection with earlier experiences or contribute insight into the nature of unconscious conflicts" (p. 168). Here we can see the framework for Ugolino's inability—or refusal—to speak his deed.

Modern psychoanalysis, through its emphasis on narcissistic states, makes a unique contribution to the understanding of the unconscious. Spotnitz (2004) says that during a state of narcissistic countertransference, "the therapist may identify with the self aspect of the [patient's] emotional experience"; in other words, "the patient's self feelings and attitudes . . . are induced in the therapist" (p. 166). So, just as the analyst's narcissistic countertransference may make sense of the unconscious emotional state of the patient, so too may Dante's reactions to Ugolino's story reveal emotions that Ugolino has induced, unconsciously, in Dante.

Dante appears to experience a narcissistic countertransference state when, during his promise to Ugolino to tell his tale, he adds a caveat: "[I]f your quarrel with him is justified,/then knowing who you are and what's his sin,/I shall repay you yet on the earth above, *if that with which I speak does not dry up*" (XXXII,137–139, italics added). It is as if, in witnessing Ugolino's gnawing away at Ruggieri's skull, Dante is induced with the same resistance as Ugolino: an incapacity—or unwill-ingness—to articulate the hideous act of cannibalism or, if it is blocked from consciousness, to become conscious of this deed. In the first case, we see the type of resistance that analysts regularly encounter with patients who do not want to verbalize a thought because of fear. In the second case, it is possible that the experience of starvation and subse-quent rage and hunger are so traumatic for Ugolino that he experiences something like a temporary psychosis that obliterates or powerfully represses the memory of violent behavior.[22] It is as if the mere act of viewing Ugolino's treatment of Ruggieri infects Dante with the same resistance that afflicts the Count. Perhaps it is not a coincidence that both the violation of the human body and the violation of the rule to speak what comes to mind involve the same agent: the mouth.

Ugolino's wiping of his mouth on the hair of his enemy also appears to serve as an unconscious communication—a kind of parapraxis of the body[23]—that reveals the degree to which Ugolino is disconnected from a conscious awareness of having cannibalized his own children. But, per-haps more importantly, Ugolino's hand points, literally, to the weapon used in the crime: his own mouth. Similarly, at the moment at which Ugolino would reveal his cannibalism, he again substitutes an action for words. His final words to Dante are, "And then, hunger overpowered grief" (XXXIII.75). Then, instead of saying explicitly that he cannibal-ized his children, "with eyes awry,/again he gripped the sad skull in his teeth,/which, like a dog's, were strong down to the bone" (XXXIII.76-78). We may hypothesize that Ugolino does not consciously realize, when he bites again into Ruggieri's skull, that he is repeating the same act which expressed, on Earth, the fact that his "hunger overpowered grief."

Ugolino's first words further establish the thematic groundwork for an understanding of his resistance to articulating his desire to cannibal-ize. By telling Dante that to speak of his past is to renew despairing pain, Ugolino echoes the language of Virgil's Aeneid, a text that, along with the Bible, is Dante's most valuable literary source. Virgil's Aeneas recalls the fall of Troy with "Infandum dolorem"[24]—that is, unspeak-able pain—so that when Ugolino talks of "disperato dolor"—despair-

---

[22]This is not unheard of; for example, it may occur in soldiers suffering from post-traumatic stress disorder who go on a "killing rampage" only to have no recollection afterwards. It may also have an analogue in the disorganization of speech, behavior, or thoughts that schizophrenics dis-play when under the pressures of their "constipated aggression" (Spotnitz, 2004). See also com-mentary from Kernberg (1995) included in this essay.

[23]Freccero (1986) comments, "Ugolino does not grasp the import of his own words" (p. 153). The same may be said here of his gestures.

[24]This is a literal translation of the Latin in Virgil's *Aeneid,* Book II, line 3. Mandelbaum (1991), in his verse translation, uses "Too terrible for tongues," Singleton (1970) uses "Beyond all words."

ing pain—he echoes the fact that the agony of having cannibalized his children is unspeakable, just as Aeneas's memory of the fall of Troy is unspeakable. Freccero (1986) goes even further: "The omission of that word [infandum] in Dante's allusion [to the *Aeneid*] seems to underscore its import in this even more terrible context. Nevertheless . . . the absence of this sign is itself significant" (p. 160). Freccero later argues that the absence of the term "infandum" (or its Italian equivalent) is a metaphor for the unspeakable nature of Ugolino's cannibalism; that is to say, the word is absent not by accident, but precisely *because* it is unspeakable. Freccero's interpretation aligns symmetrically with the psychoanalytic notion of a "resistance" as a force which keeps something absent, unspoken.

The ambiguity of Ugolino's final statement may also reveal his unconscious wish to preserve his children within himself. In the same way that his physical hunger overpowers the grief he feels for his dead children, we may also see that incorporating the "good objects" embodied by his children overpowers the intense feelings of grief—or, to put it another way, the experience of "bad objects"—that plague Ugolino, almost as if he were attempting to ingest an antidote. Abraham (1924) confirms as much when he cites the case of a severely depressed widower who dreamed he cannibalized his wife and, in doing so, restored her to life. Likewise, the Catholic notion of the Holy Eucharist as the "living bread" of Jesus Christ reiterates the same idea—that by eating the flesh of the good object we can somehow restore ourselves to life.

Finally, I would comment on two specific points in Freccero's (1986) "Bestial Sign and Bread of Angels." First, Freccero writes of Ugolino, "Because [he] is a literalist . . . he cannot understand the spiritual significance of [his sons'] apparently literal statement [to eat their flesh]" (p. 161). Why is Ugolino a literalist? The psychoanalytic response might be something like the following: At the moment when his libido can no longer bind his rage—that is to say, at the moment that the schizophrenic defense breaks down—Ugolino becomes psychotic. His dream, like all dreams, is a kind of temporary psychosis; when he wakes and finds that his situation cannot improve, actual psychosis overtakes him, revealing no difference between the wish and the action, between the symbol and the meaning. In other words, the actions conform to a literal understanding of his sons' earlier words because, in his state of psychosis, he no longer is able to hear his sons' words symbolically. Lacan's (Leader, 2000) notion of "foreclosure" clarifies this mechanism: "When an element is foreclosed, it can't return to the symbolic. . . . It returns not in the symbolic, but in the real" (p. 107). This represents the Lacanian concept of psychosis. Ugolino's desire cannot be symbolized—as a dream, or otherwise. "It would be far less painful for us if/you ate of us" (61–62) becomes a literal request to him, reflective of his literal desire to cannibalize.

Second, Freccero (1986) states, "The absence of a sign . . . must be construed as a sign" (p. 162). We might take this as another way of saying something familiar to any psychoanalyst: The resistance to speaking is itself a symbolic communication. Therefore, Ugolino's silence at the end of his tale stands in the place of something he is leaving unspoken—cannibalism.

Conclusion

We may think of Ugolino as the patient who continually fails to break the pattern of his repetition compulsion despite the presence of an analyst. His children, seeing his debilitating rage, offer themselves as food, but Ugolino forgets the fundamental rule: words, not actions, embody the highest human expression. It is as if the analyst has said to the chronically rageful patient (often enough a schizophrenic), "Attack me, *using words*, not yourself." Had Ugolino shared his frustration with his sons, he might then have been able to overcome the resistance which kept him silent; then, perhaps, he might have died in communion with them. Instead, by cannibalizing them, Ugolino guarantees that he will forever be forced to repeat his compulsion in the lowest circle of Hell. There, he is literally frozen in place, unable to make new choices as he repeats endlessly the very act that symbolizes his inner torture. When the opportunity to overcome his resistance presents itself again, in the form of Dante—interlocutor-cum-psychoanalyst—Ugolino still cannot break the bonds of his repetition compulsion.

In the simplest sense, this merely means that the gratification obtained from the repetition must exceed Ugolino's expectations of what his sons or Dante can possibly offer him. But in another, more important, sense Ugolino's punishment also highlights Dante's conviction that truly empathic human interaction—epitomized by the analytic dyad—can save us. Freccero (1986) says that Ugolino's "tragedy is a failure of interpretation" (p. 157), and this may very well be said of all the sinners in *Inferno*: they have failed to understand the unconscious dynamics driving them to sins which result in their eternal damnation. Seen from a psychoanalytic standpoint, *Inferno* serves not just as Dante's mystical religious vision of Hell; it is also an expression of Dante's own intrapsychic processes. What damns us, from Dante's perspective, is our failure to live our lives mediated by a truly empathic relationship to another human being. As Freccero writes, the Ugolino episode dramatizes the conceptualization of all of *Inferno*: "the alternatives are narrowed down to two in man's relationship to his fellow man: communion or cannibalism" (p. 153). So, for example, in failing to conceive of her relationship with Paolo as anything more than a gratification of her own body's desire, Francesca di Rimini lands herself in Hell (Canto V). Similarly, Ulysses, incapable of acknowledging the humanity of his shipmates, instead seeks to aggrandize his own ego; as a consequence he destroys everyone through his hubris (Canto XXVI). Ultimately, Ugolino represents the nadir of such destructive narcissism.

In other words, sin, for Dante, may be characterized as negative narcissism while virtue can be seen as the conscious striving to appreciate the separateness and integrity of the other. In an analysis, this process begins when the analyst is able to interpret the transference and resistance as well as make proper sense of his own countertransference and countertransference resistance. In the end, though, the analyst can only do so much. Eventually it is up to the patient to recognize that he can often be opportunistic in his reactions to the analyst, turning the analyst into something from his own past rather than seeing the analyst as a separate person.

It is not coincidental that Dante the Pilgrim can only survive the passage through Hell with the help of his guide, Virgil. Similarly, the patient can make it through the "hell" of his unconscious only through the help of the analyst. Jung (1969) once wrote of the struggle to understand the self:

> In the end, one has to admit that there are problems which one simply cannot solve on one's own resources. . . . We should never forget that in dealing with the [the darkest regions of the mind], we are dealing with psychic facts which have never been in man's possession before, since they were always found "outside" his psychic territory. (p. 21, 28)

Psychoanalysis provides us the means to explore this territory safely.

REFERENCES

Abraham, K. (1924), A short study of the development of the libido, viewed in the light of mental disorders. *Selected Papers of Karl Abraham*. New York: Brunner/Mazel, 1979.

Ahern, John (1998), Amphion and the poetics of retaliation. *Lectura Dantis: Inferno*. Mandelbaum, A., A. Oldcorn & C. Ross, eds. Berkeley: University of California Press.

Chiarenza, M. M. (1989), *The Divine Comedy: Tracing God's Art*. Boston: Twain Publishers.

D'Amato, B. (2002), Defensive meaning in a schizophrenic patient's preoccupation with other therapists. *Modern Pyschoanalysis*, 27:133–158.

Freccero, J. (1986), *Dante: The Poetics of Conversion*. Cambridge, MA: Harvard University Press.

Freeman, R. & T. Freeman (1992), An anatomical commentary on the concept of infantile oral sadism. *International Journal of Psychoanalysis*, 73:343–348.

Freud, S. (1900), The interpretation of dreams. *Standard Edition*. London: Hogarth Press, 4 & 5.

———— (1905), Three essays on the theory of sexuality. *Standard Edition*. London: Hogarth Press, 7:125–245.

———— (1913), Totem and taboo. *Standard Edition*. London: Hogarth Press, 13:1–162.

———— (1920), Beyond the pleasure principle. *Standard Edition*. London: Hogarth Press, 18:1–64

Herzman, R. (1980), Cannibalism and communion in *Inferno* XXXIII. *Dante Studies*, 98:53–78.

Hinshelwood, R. D. (1991), *A Dictionary of Kleinian Thought*. Second Edition. Northvale, NJ: Jason Aronson.

Hollander, R. (2000), *The Inferno*. New York: Doubleday.

Jung, C. G. (1969), *The Archetypes and the Collective Unconscious*. Second Edition. R. F. C. Hull, translator. Princeton, NJ: Princeton University Press.

Kernberg, O. (1995), Aggression and transference in severe personality disorders. *Psychiatric Times*, Feb. 1995.

Klein, M. (1930), The importance of symbol formation in the development of the ego. *The Selected Melanie Klein*. J. Mitchell, ed. New York: Free Press, 1987.

———— (1956)."A study of envy and gratitude. The importance of symbol formation in the development of the ego. *The Selected Melanie Klein*. J. Mitchell, ed. New York: Free Press, 1987.

Leader, D. & J. Groves (2000), *Introducing Lacan*. London: Icon Books.

Luke, H. (1989), *Dark Wood to White Rose: Journey and Transformation in Dante's Divine Comedy*. New York: Parabola Books.

Mandelbaum, A., translator (1971), *The Aeneid of Virgil*. New York: Bantam.

———— ed. & translator (1981), *Inferno*. New York: Bantam.

McDougall, J. (1995), The smell self and the skin self. *The Many Faces of Eros*. New York: W. W. Norton.

Meadow, P. W. (2003), *The New Psychoanalysis*. Lanham, MD: Rowman & Littlefield.

Moore, B. & B. Fine (1990), *Psychoanalytic Terms & Concepts*. New Haven, CT: Yale University Press.

Phillips, A. (1998), *The Beast in the Nursery: On Curiosity and Other Appetites*. New York: Random House.

Singleton, J. (1970), *The Divine Comedy: Translated, with a Commentary*. Princeton, NJ: Princeton University Press.

Spotnitz, H. (2004), *Modern Psychoanalysis of the Schizophrenic Patient*. 2004 Second Edition. New York: YBK.

Spotnitz, H. & P. W. Meadow (1995), *Treatment of the Narcissistic Neuroses*. Revised Edition. Northvale, NJ: Aronson.

Winnicott, D.W. (1986), *Home is Where We Start From*. New York: W. W. Norton.

55 East 84th Street
New York NY 10028
ctalbot@regis-nyc.org

Modern Psychoanalysis
Vol. XXX, No. 1, 2005

Book Reviews

On the Freud Watch: Public Memoirs. **Paul Roazen. London: Free Association Books, 2003. 224 pp.**

Any text or work can be read in many different ways. Different readers meet different writers in a text. Similar to writing, reading may be considered to a great extent as autobiographical. Although we like to think of the reality of the text regardless of the reader, we can never be certain that we are not reading our own thoughts into someone else's words. Having said all of this, I find *On the Freud Watch* an outstanding piece of work. It is a pleasure trip through personally selected psychiatric and psychoanalytic scenes. It is a trip of recovery—re-finding—rather than of discovery or finding. Even if one does not recall being in those affective spaces, one gets a feeling of déjà vu.

I could talk all about the content of the book, which consists of 13 lively chapters and an intimately elegant personal epilogue. Yet, I find the process of the way the book unfolds even more fascinating. I find the book to proceed like a mini-analysis in 14 sessions. It is a mini-analysis based on the hope of bringing closure to some nagging unfinished business in the past. A nagging business may never be finished in a time-limited analysis, but nevertheless Paul Roazen walks out of the book content and serene. (Paul Roazen read an early draft of this review before his death on November 3, 2005.)The original analysis had been entered into for the sake of discovering the ultimate scandalous secret of an important historical object, Sigmund Freud. Since the ultimate scandalous secret—similar to Lacanian desire—can never be discovered, we go through life discovering smaller secrets which are momentarily satisfying without quenching our thirst for the ultimate one. Throughout this written analysis, Roazen is in a dialogue with the representation of two unsavory "objects," which is what he calls Kurt E. Eissler and Anna Freud. He uses many sessions (chapters) fighting with them. He seems narcissistically injured by them. They seem to have made a lot of noise to obliterate his attempt to make a symbolic contact with Freud. Roazen tries to process the injury out of his psyche over and over again. Following him through his emotionally charged dialogue, I found myself trying to do my regular interventions, saying, "So what?" "Who gives a damn about Kurt Eissler and Anna Freud these days?" "Paul, why are you taking their past noises so personally?" Yet, I managed to shut up and let him work through his trauma himself. Since he is being authentic rather than an "as-if" character, it is very easy to feel what he feels, or to feel what you feel he feels.

His reminiscences of his early days hanging around the old Massachusetts Mental Health Center bring back my own old memories, making me nostalgic for my own macabre experience of doing internships at a private and at a state mental hospital in Massachusetts in the '80s. I also had much difficulty telling the difference between the patients and the clinical staff. I'll never forget Marshal, a bright black man who was suddenly shipped to Bridgewater State Hospital because he had allegedly threatened to stab a young beautiful white female social worker with a pencil. I used to think he was a psychiatric social worker until I was told by a psychologist that the man was a delusional psychotic. His delusion, according to the psychologist, was that "he thought he was a Black Muslim." Since for some reason in that psychologist's mind he couldn't have *been* a Black Muslim, the "false belief" that he *was* a Black Muslim helped form his diagnosis of paranoid schizophrenic. The chief psychologist at that unit happened to be also an ordained minister. The bumper sticker on the back of her station wagon read: *Jesus is my Co-Pilot.*

Roazen's short reference to the "hippie" girl who had been diagnosed as schizophrenic because the resident disapproved of her behavior and her hair style, reminded me of poor Mr. Ferdinand who had been brought in by the police looking lost and confused. He quickly received a diagnosis of schizophrenia with a differential diagnosis of brain injury. No one could understand what he was babbling about. He had to be let out the following week when his daughter showed up to claim her Portuguese dad who had got lost and happened not to know even a single word of English. It was here that I suddenly took notice of my own countertransferential fantasies having left Roazen to go back to re-find my own past. The elicited memories/fantasies say as much about him as about me. It speaks, I believe, to Paul Roazen's rejection of authority, to his idealization of the underdog, to his dislike for institutional psychiatry, to his contempt for trivialization or medicalization of the human condition, to his lack of tolerance for force feeding of dogma in the name of truth, to his dislike of gatekeepers, and to his romantic wish to see the world uncontaminated by the boring adult sensibilities—the way it is seen by a child. Roazen's passionate admiration for Ferenczi, Rank, and Rycroft fall within that affective space. I should confess that I do not understand where in his psyche his love for Carl Jung originates. It is here that I fall out of tune with him. He is still somewhat religious and a bit mystic.

I love the session when he talks about Charles Rycroft. His expression of pleasure over paying tribute to such an original psychoanalyst is edifying. Here he focuses on Rycroft's paper, "On Ablation of Parental Images *or* the Illusion of Having Created Oneself." This had been a politically incorrect paper about a group of patients who chose to disown their past. The paper turned out to describe many analysts, or many of those who aspire to become analysts, better than it described some of the patients. Psychoanalysis, according to Rycroft, "has a special attraction for people whose own relationship to their bodies and their past is ambiguous and whose own inner frames of reference are ill-defined" (p. 32). The paper goes further to throw light on proselytizing tendencies of different psychoanalytic schools and on their inability to enter into an open discourse with one another over theoretical differences. He quotes directly from Rycroft:

> Patients and student analysands who do in fact succeed in being analyzed by the analyst of their own choice often, it seems to me, become proselytizers of their analyst's theories as much out of personal vanity as out of genuine appreciation and gratitude for his understanding and skill. In such cases the patient or analysand patronizes his analyst, while basking in the reflected glory of someone whom he has himself elected to idealize and whom he believes he has discovered; thereby reversing the humiliating biological fact that he did not choose his own parents (p. 31).

The chapter is an interesting portrayal of petty personal, interpersonal, and organizational politics that serve the purpose of giving birth to a particular group. Roazen tries desperately not to fall into the cast of such characters. There is no way for him to close the door to the past where he has buried many precious secrets.

Session after session, chapter after chapter, through Charles Dickens's *David Copperfield* and Eugene O'Neill's *Long Day's Journey into Night*, Roazen finally arrives comfortably at his own fantastic past. The Personal Epilogue: Secret Spaces flows smoothly in the last session—serves as the last movement of this personal symphony. He seems to have achieved some resolution, at least momentarily. This I should say comes after his reflection on Freud's tolerance for fault and marginality as well as his therapeutic philosophy that people have to learn how to live with pain and distress rather than being "cured" of their existential condition.

> They say best men are molded out of fault,
> And, for the most, become much more the better
> For being a little bad. (p. 212)

Paul Roazen has given us another piece of scholarship that speaks loudly to the interaction between history and biography. I very much like the author of this text. Roazen loves psychoanalysis. Although Anna Freud had called him "a menace [in] whatever he writes" (p. 37), he is a friend of psychoanalysis. And his contribution to psychoanalysis is much more significant than those whose thoughts are "deformed by personal vanity or ideological piety." Even if some orthodox analysts want to regard him as an enemy of psychoanalysis—and I have heard this remark made about him by a few analytic colleagues—he is an intelligent and thoughtful "enemy," which, according to a Persian proverb, is much better than a stupid friend, who always undermines us through his or her ignorant "kind" contribution.

I feel that while Roazen, rightfully I believe, criticizes psychoanalysts from a postmodern epistemological stand—that they continue "to talk naively about Freud's 'discoveries,' as if what were at issue were 'facts' rather than new ways of looking at things," he becomes an historical realist when he talks about his own "discoveries." When it comes to his own (re)findings, he treats them as historical rather than as narrative truth. He believes that as a "distant communicator of historical discoveries," he has been fortunate to stumble on some objective facts (p. 58). Paul Roazen knows very well that what historians or news reporters do—despite their claims to "objectivity"—is to *make* news or *construct* history rather than to stumble upon historical truth. Although I like Roazen's reconstruction of Victor Tausk's suicide much better than Eissler's pompous story, I consider both of them to qualify as narrative truth.

I should admit that if I were looking around for some juicy exotic material to discover, I wouldn't have emotionally run into Freud's analysis of his own daughter, Anna. I would not have found it that interesting. The story wouldn't have touched a sensitive spot in my soul.

What is it about the analysis of a daughter by a father that is a cardinal sin, unethical, unprofessional, or even incestuous? And so what if it were judged to be all of the above? For psychoanalysis that aims to transcend—and in fact neutralize—the "neurotic" moral demands, this narrative lacks much excitement. Different socio-emotional detectives may discover (construct) different crimes.

Roazen tries to trace the origin of the requirement of analytic training in order to become an analyst to Jung. This attempt, I believe, is almost pre-Nietzscheian. How can we trace the "real" author of a text outside its cultural and intellectual surroundings? How can we trace the "originality" of an idea in a mind which is dialogically constructed? Would Jung have stumbled over the requirement of analytic training if he had not met Freud and had not been exposed to Freud's idea of psychoanalysis? I have repeatedly heard from some analysts or analytic candidates that their patients steal their dreams or their fantasies. My question has always been: who steals whose fantasies? In the spirit of Socratic Method of psychoanalysis, it is not the analyst who tells the analysand the answer to her questions; it is the analysand who "stumbles" onto the answers by the analyst's repeated questioning.

In this book, Roazen comes across again as a nonconformist and a skeptic. He holds "the liberal conviction that all power needs to be questioned. And so the recommendation that seems to [him] most apt is that we pursue a counter-cyclical approach, which means skepticism about the present and special generosity about the easily forgotten past" (p. 198). But then he becomes patriotic and a bit incensed by Freud's anti-Americanism. To him, Freud used America as an object for his projections. In a letter to Ferenczi, Freud had complained about the tendency of the American press to fabricate news, a charge that one hears even today from people all over the world. Freud had also said some unkind words about the American empty rhetoric of freedom. He had even suggested that "the Statue of Liberty in New York harbor should be replaced by a monkey holding up a Bible" (p. 127). Roazen finds this remark to be racist. However, his interpretation of the metaphor "monkey" is itself curious. If a monkey with a Bible is taken to represent a mindless conformity and an evangelical zeal, it would even speak to today's social and political scene. Here one may insert a caveat that today "the monkey" itself is being driven out of Darwin's theory of evolution by the moral majority in America in favor of Adam and Eve.

I cannot praise Roazen enough for his keen observation on the dynamics of power in psychiatry, psychoanalysis, and history. He is sensitive to the nuances of power in the structure of human relationship. He might have gone a bit farther and embraced the sociological sense of power, according to which every relationship is an equation of power. Roazen's own pursuit of historical "truth" in psychoanalysis can be easily unpacked in terms of power. A question that I once asked him in one of his monthly dinner and discussion seminars in Cambridge was: "What do you think is your 'unconscious' motivation for writing about important people?"

Siamak Movahedi

THE ANALYST'S ANALYST WITHIN. **Lora Heims Tessman. Hillsdale, NJ: The Analytic Press, 2003. 363 pp.**

This study is about post-termination recollections of their analyses by 34 practicing analysts, 30 from the Boston Psychoanalytic Institute and four from outside that area. Several questions guided the research: "success" of analysis; the role of gender; attitudes of the analyst toward the analysand; what attributes of the analyst were linked to change; post-analytic contacts with the analyst; and whether practice theories at the time affected the analytic experience. The total number of analyses studied was 64 because 28 of the 34 participants had two or more analyses. Gender effects were studied by comparing same-sex and opposite-sex analyst–patient dyads.

The research protocol included 13 penetrating questions, which were sent to potential participants in preparation for interviews. For example, "How would you describe the inner presence of your analyst around the time of termination; how did that change over the years; how is that now?" And, "What forms of loving and/or hating, missing or desiring, wanting to be loved, or to be appreciated and respected by your analyst continue to have their momentum, and how? Did you and do you now have fantasies or wishes for some sort of eventual friendship with your analyst? Did you have longings to empathically know the flux of your analyst's own inner emotional life and do you now?" (p. 321)

Taped interviews lasted two to eight hours, as questions were explored in detail. Confidentiality was protected by participants' choosing their own code names, reviewing their transcripts for consent to publish, and being able to delete sensitive material and identifying data. After transcription, all tapes were destroyed to avoid voice recognition.

Once transcribed and tabulated, the responses were grouped into three categories: degree of retrospective satisfaction with the analysis; gender combination effects; and the decade in which the analysis took place.

Degree of satisfaction
- 25 or 39% of the 64 analyses were described as deeply satisfying.
- 25 or 39% of the 64 analyses were moderately satisfying.
- 14 or 22% of the 64 analyses were described as dissatisfying.

Gender and Satisfaction with the Analysis
The highest incidence of satisfaction occurs for males with female analysts and females with male analysts. The highest incidence of dissatisfaction was for male patients with male analysts.

Decade of Analysis and Satisfaction Rating
Participants were more likely to be dissatisfied with analyses conducted
between 1965 and 1975, but 10 times more likely to be deeply satisfied
with experiences between 1985 and 1995.

Tessman recognizes that selective memory highlights certain aspects
of the earlier analysis. However, she also notes that the effects of an
analysis may be ongoing, with changes occurring over time. She sites
Guntrip, who in 1975 advised analysts to be open to post-analytic
improvements and not to expect the full work of analysis to be accomplished before termination. For some decades it was assumed that, in a
successful analysis, the analysand worked through the transference to
independence from attachment to the analyst and parents. The next step
was self-analysis, aided by identification with the analyst. The final
phase was mourning the loss of the analyst as a *person.*

In contrast, more recent assumptions about termination focus on the
concept of internalization. "In this view what is internalized are transformed anticipations, in the form of representation, verbal and nonverbal, of both dyadic interchange and self-contained states in the presence
of the other" (p. 9). In short, "it is not the interaction in itself that
remains memorable, but the intrapsychic representation of that interaction. As the analysis progresses and self-protective maneuvers lend less
coloration to the image of the analyst, the analysand increasingly experiences the actuality of the analyst" (p. 9).

As termination approaches, the relationship shifts from focus on the
patient's inner world to a growing sense of mutuality with the analyst.
The working-through process includes "the patient's heightened ability
to get a sense of the analyst's functional person, his strength and weakness. . . . (I)n so doing the patient can get out of a more infantilized,
idealizing position in relation to the analyst" (Cooper, [2000], qtd. in
Miller, p. 10).

In this view, transference, defined as distortion of the real analyst
functioning as a blank screen, is redefined as memories and affects that
are transformed by realistic appraisal of the analyst rather than by automatic repetition.

The analyst/analysand subjects who considered their own analyses
successful cited the following factors: having feelings of freedom and

having the ability to love and to hate, to feel authentic rather than automatically adaptive, to feel understood rather than unseen for who they were, and to feel cared for, even loved, rather than shamed or unworthy of wanting to have some personal significance to the analyst. Tessman concludes that transferences and memories continue long after the analysis has terminated and that the more "positive" the analytic experience was, the more vivid the analyst's inner presence. Very significant for a positive analytic experience was recalling the analyst as "a complete other, a person in his or her own right, with a good life of his own," not in need of being filled with love, recognition, and admiration from analysands.

However, the loved analyst's "real" behavior (not fitting the transferential wishes of the patient) may create feelings of dissonance and even diminish love yearnings from the past. The up side of this, according to Tessman, is making the analysand more open to the present. "Then the analyst within, not born of illusion, can partake in generative collusion" (p. 317). Tessman refers to Winnicott's (1960) idea that feeling authentic means recognizing an outside reality that is not one's own projection, not "mirroring," but contacting other minds. In effect, the projected other created by the self has to be mentally destroyed in order to appreciate the other, in this case the analyst, as a separate, living being who can participate in one's life.

Looking at many chapters with quoted statements of both the participants and the researcher, this reviewer was struck with how these intimate discussions brought up unresolved issues and feelings that Tessman helped to interpret and resolve with her leading questions and clarifying interpretations. This mixture, although perhaps hard to avoid with these experienced analysts, tends to muddy the research aspects. Viewed as a set of clinical narratives, the work makes the reader privy to inner thoughts of the subjects about the analytic process, as well as to what they tend to remember, regret, profit from, resent, and wish they had known about the analyst—a whole mosaic of issues raised by the analytic experiences that continue to be reviewed and revised by the participants' self-analyses. Whether the analyst had been helpful or not, remembered positively or not, was linked to how understood the analysand felt, and this varied considerably. Special problems such as the illness of the analyst and sudden "schizoid withdrawals" by the analyst were cited as particularly difficult.

In summary, Tessman's book is filled with narrative, interpretation, and integration of literature with the many themes raised by this ambitious look at post-termination phenomena. For the practicing analyst and analytic student alike it illuminates interchanges that will resonate with one's own experiences on or in back of the couch. As a clinical study rather than a controlled research endeavor, it is well worth a detailed read to see how these sophisticated analysts evaluated their own experiences as analysands.

Marjorie E. Kettell

Books Received

Akhtar, Salman & Harold Blum, eds. *The Language of Emotions: Development, Psychopathology, and Technique*. Lanham, MD: Rowman & Littlefield, 2005. 192 pp. softcover

Binder, Jeffrey L. *Key Competencies in Brief Dynamic Psychotherapy: Clinical Practice Beyond the Manual*. New York: Guilford Press, 2005. 290 pp.

Bridges, Nancy A. *Moving beyond the Comfort Zone in Psychotherapy*. Lanham, MD: Jason Aronson, 2005. 196 pp.

Caplan, Paula J. & Lisa Cosgrove, eds. *Bias in Psychiatric Disgnosis*. Lanham, MD: Jason Aronson, 2004. 269 pp. softcover.

Gabbard, Glen O. *Psychodynamic Psychiatry*. Fourth Edition. Washington, DC: American Psychiatric Publishing, 2005. 629 pp.

Jordan, Judith V., Maureen Walker & Linda M. Hartling. *The Complexity of Connection*. New York: The Guilford Press, 2004. 308 pp. softcover.

Lenzenweger, Mark F. & John F. Clarkin. *Major Theories of Personality Disorder*. New York: The Guilford Press, 2005. 464 pp.

Miller, Jacques-Alain. *The Pathology of Democracy: A Letter to Bernard Accoyer and to Enlightened Opinion*. New York: Karnac, 2005. 72 pp. paperback.

Molino, Anthony, ed. *Culture, Subject, Psyche: Dialogues in Psychoanalysis and Anthropology*. Middletown, CT: Wesleyan University Press, 2004. 217 pp. paperback.

Mollon, Phil. *EMDR and the Energy Therapies*. New York: Karnac, 2005. 313 pp. softcover.

Paris, Joel. *The Fall of an Icon: Psychoanalysis and Academic Psychiatry*. Toronto: University of Toronto Press, 2005. 226 pp. softcover.

Person, Ethel S., Arnold M. Cooper & Glen O. Gabbard, eds. *Textbook of Psychoanalysis*. Washington, DC: American Psychiatric Publishing, 2005. 602 pp.

Shamdasani, Sonu. *Jung Stripped Bare: By His Biographers, Even*. New York: Karnac, 2005. 132 pp. softcover.

Schoenewolf, Gerald. *111 Common Therapeutic Blunders*. Second Edition. Lanham, MD: Rowman & Littlefield, 2005. 360 pp. softcover.

Yalom, Irvin D. *The Schopenhauer Cure*. New York: HarperCollins, 2004. 358 pp.

Weinger, Marcella Bakur, Paul C. Cooper, & Claude Barbre. *Psychotherapy and Religion*. New York: Jason Aronson, 2005. 293 pp.

Wishnie, Howard A. *Working in the Countertransference: Necessary Entanglements*. Lanham, MD: Rowman & Littlefield, 2005. 263 pp.

About the Authors

D'AMATO, BARBARA, M.A., is a psychoanalyst in private practice in New York City and in Brooklyn. She is a member of the faculty of the Center for Modern Psychoanalytic Studies, where she is a training analyst and supervisor. She is researching the dreams of adult adoptees as a doctoral candidate at the Cyril Z. Meadow Institute.

GELTNER, PAUL, D.S.W., is the director of training at the Psychoanalytic Psychotherapy Study Center. He has published papers on dreams, countertransference, child analysis, and evolutionary psychology. He is in private practice in New York City and Brooklyn, specializing in mood and learning disorders and in individual and group supervision.

GILHOOLEY, DAN, M.A., is a graduate of and fellow at the Center for Modern Psychoanalytic Studies. He is a professor at Suffolk County Community College, where he was also Dean. He is a recipient of Vermont Association for Psychoanalytic Studies Research Award and NAAP Gradiva Award for Art. In 1991, he was elected to the National Academy of Design. Mr Gilhooley has had 18 one-person exhibitions and has participated in over 120 group shows nationally. He is in private practice in New York City and Bellport, NY.

LAQUERCIA, THEODORE, Ph.D., is a training and supervising analyst at the Center for Modern Psychoanalytic Studies and the Boston Graduate School of Psychoanalysis and maintains a practice in New York and Boston. He is a vice president of the Society of Modern Psychoanalysts and coordinates their national and international confer-

© 2005 CMPS/*Modern Psychoanalysis*, Vol. 30, No. 1

ences. He is a former president of the Boston Center for Modern Psychoanalytic Studies and has chaired accreditation committees for the National Association for the Advancement of Psychoanalysis and the Society of Modern Psychoanalysts and has done extensive work in curriculum studies and standards in psychoanalytic training.

POLLACK-GOMOLIN, ROBIN, Psya.D., is a graduate of Boston Graduate School of Psychoanalysis and received her Psya.D. from The Institute for the Study of Violence. She is a part-time faculty member at the University of Massachusetts, Boston, in both the psychology and sociology departments and was recently appointed to the faculty of Boston Graduate School of Psychoanalysis.

SHEPHERD, MARY, M.A., is a training and supervising analyst and an associate professor at the Boston Graduate School of Psychoanalysis, where she is also the public information officer. She has written on modern psychoanalytic history and anaclitic countertransference considerations. Her current research interest involves the attempt to integrate aspects of psychoanalytic metatheory with the recent discoveries of neuroscience.

TALBOT, CHRISTIAN, B.A., teaches English literature at Regis High School in Manhattan and is a master's degree candidate at the Boston Graduate School of Psychoanalysis–New York. He was awarded a grant from the National Endowment for the Humanities in 2000 to study Shakespeare at the Folger Shakespeare Library, where he published lesson plans for teachers of *Macbeth* and *King Lear*. He is currently writing his master's thesis on Islamic extremism.

Printed in the United States
43772LVS00002B/1-102